Paradise Lost A TERCENTENARY TRIBUTE

Papers given at the
Conference on the
Tercentenary of *Paradise Lost*
University of Western Ontario
October 1967

PUBLISHED BY UNIVERSITY OF TORONTO PRESS
IN ASSOCIATION WITH
THE UNIVERSITY OF WESTERN ONTARIO

Paradise Lost

A TERCENTENARY TRIBUTE

EDITED BY BALACHANDRA RAJAN

CONTENTS

CONTRIBUTORS

Roy Daniells

University Professor of English Language and Literature at the University of British Columbia and the author of *Milton Mannerism and Baroque* (1963). He has edited Thomas Traherne's *A Serious and Pathetic Contemplation of the Mercies of God* (1941) and has published two volumes of poetry, *Deeper Into the Forest* (1948) and *The Chequered Shade* (1963).

Northrop Frye

University Professor at the University of Toronto. Among his many books are *Fearful Symmetry* (1947), *The Anatomy of Criticism* (1957), *Fables of Identity* (1963), *The Well-Tempered Critic* (1963), *The Educated Imagination* (1963), *T. S. Eliot* (1963), *A Natural Perspective* (1965), *Fools of Time* (1967), and *The Modern Century* (1967). *The Return to Eden* (1965) is a study of Milton's two epics.

Arthur E. Barker

Professor of English at the University of Illinois. He is the author of *Milton and the Puritan Dilemma* (1942) and has edited *Milton: Modern Essays in Criticism* (1965).

Hugh MacCallum

Associate Professor of English at the University of Toronto. He has published articles on Milton and sacred history and on Milton and figurative interpretation of the Bible.

Balachandra Rajan

Senior Professor of English at the University of Western Ontario and the author of *"Paradise Lost" and the Seventeenth Century Reader* (1947) and of *W. B. Yeats: a Critical Introduction* (1965). He has edited books on *T. S. Eliot* (1947) and on *Modern American Poetry* (1950) and has published two novels, *The Dark Dancer* (1958) and *Too Long in the West* (1961).

FOREWORD

Tercentenaries have been observed in the past, but 1967
was a year in which a poem was honoured even more than its
author. Perhaps the emphasis indicates the right priority;
even if it does not, it still testifies to the relevance of *Paradise
Lost* and to its singular hold on contemporary scholarship.

Nineteen sixty-seven was the centenary of Confederation
as well as the tercentenary of Milton's epic. Opinions may
differ as to what is implied by this Pythagorean harmony.
But whatever may be the significance of the coincidence, it
seemed to us to be a good enough basis on which to allow
Canadian scholarship to pay its tribute to *Paradise Lost*. This
book consists of the papers read at a conference of Milton
scholars associated with Canadian universities, held at the
University of Western Ontario on October 19 and 20, 1967.
No attempt has been made to edit the occasion out of exis-
tence and the papers are reproduced in the order in which
they were read.

Fifteen Canadian universities sent representatives to the Conference and six American universities joined us on this occasion. In the absence of papers by scholars such as Douglas Bush, Watson Kirkconnell, Malcolm Mackenzie Ross, Ernest Sirluck, and E. J. Sprott, it cannot be said that this book is representative of the full range of Canadian Milton scholarship; but the papers printed do give some indication of the quality and variety of that scholarship.

The Canadian shelf in a Milton library should be more than interesting and some of the books on it ought to be well-thumbed. But though the situation may have changed by the time this book is published, the pioneering and compendious work of the greatest of Canadian Miltonists is not at the moment on the shelf. If the responses to Milton's poem which are printed in this collection reflect anything in common other than the poem itself, it is surely the presence of the Woodhouse tradition. That tradition began and ended in attention to the work but required that attention to be properly educated by careful schooling in the inherited form, the intellectual content, and the pattern and style of the oeuvre. In a widely known essay on the historical method, Woodhouse's description of that method is sufficiently ample to allow these various "approaches" full play in the accurate reconnaissance of the poem. What the various papers in this book have in common is the firm recognition that the text does not stand alone but is illuminated by and illuminates a properly chosen context.

Paradise Lost can be thought of as an infinite receptacle, unique as it were in its capacity for relevance. The various contributors to this volume choose different ways in which to surround the text. Professor Daniells leads us from architecture into architectonics. Professor Frye leads us back from the poem's structure into the primary structures of myth. Professor Barker sees the poem taking its shape and finding its fulfilment as the dynamic embodiment of the great theme of Christian liberty. Professor MacCallum instructs us in the background of the poem's dogma so that we can better understand some of its drama. The editor's essay is part of an attempt to look at the web of interconnectedness which the poem builds and manipulates in relation to inherited traditions and the personal tradition of the oeuvre. It is a tribute to the poem that such diversity does not result in confusion, or the "impetuous recoil" of method clashing against method. If the poem is surrounded in a way that is responsive to it, the encirclement will be taken into the field of force of the work, orienting it so as to declare something about its nature. The safeguard lies in the word "responsive," for a context must to some extent be reached for by the poetry if it is to reach back into the poem's deed of coherence.

Of many volumes on the tercentenary, this is probably the last. It is hoped that it will bring to a close, more usefully than Belial, a procession which is at least not lacking in good intentions. Having said this, it remains only to thank the University of Western Ontario for providing the facilities for this conference and for the grant which made possible the publication of this book. Since the editor is not Canadian (though associated with a Canadian university) his satisfaction in the result can at least be impartial.

The poetry throughout is cited from the Columbia edition. Where possible, the prose is cited from the Yale edition, referred to as *Prose Works*. Prose not so far published in the Yale edition is cited from the Columbia edition, referred to as *Works*.

B.R.

London, Ontario
July 1968

Paradise Lost A TERCENTENARY TRIBUTE

A HAPPY RURAL SEAT OF
VARIOUS VIEW

ROY DANIELLS

I am honoured in being the first to address this gathering of kindred souls come to pay homage to Milton. Our symposium, however, is more Shakespearean than Miltonic in its plan. This paper will not, like *Paradise Lost*'s opening, strike resonant chords evoking all that is to come or act as an overture anticipating the dominant themes. On the contrary, it will resemble a brief first scene in the playhouse, in which some minor happenings establish a mood and allow the audience time to finish the apple it is eating and settle down.

My theme is the pleasure of living in the Garden of Eden, the skill with which Milton has managed its aspect and its prospect, the care with which he has provided everything Adam and Eve can require. They are our first parents, our archetypal selves; it is really for us he has made all these arrangements.

It is a walled garden, *hortus conclusus*, protected and self-contained. Yet, by a variety of means, all sense of being closed in claustrophobically is avoided. The wall is varied in structure. Stupendously towering in alabaster cliffs in one part, it turns elsewhere into an immense, forested acclivity crowned by a hedge of verdure. When looked up to from the outside, it suggests a castle dominating the landscape. Adam, from the inside, can look out but never approaches the wall, never leans out like the Blessd Damozel. As a consequence, he never seems bounded or limited in his movements.

On the eastern side, there is a gate, between whose rocky pillars "*Gabriel* sat / Chief of th' Angelic Guards." (IV, 549–50) I used to think Milton had been a little awkward in providing a gate only for the expulsion of Adam and Eve. But not so. It is used. Raphael lights on the eastern cliff of Paradise and comes in through the portal. In fact, he reviews the guard: "Strait knew him all the Bands / Of angels under watch; and to his state. And to his message high in honour rise / ... Thir glittering Tents he passd." (V, 287–91) Here also Uriel makes his landing, "gliding through the Eeven / On a Sun-beam." (IV, 555–6) Adam and Eve live under an open sky from which beneficent beings appear, but the archangels do not merely drop in. Arrivals are carefully controlled, a superb sense of order reigns, and the privacy of the human pair is never invaded.

Within the garden there is a beautiful handling of spatial relations, although no plan appears to suggest rigidity or limits. The bower is shaded and retired; we are never told precisely where it is in relation to anything else. The scene, unmapped, combines effects of ornamental planting with pastoral landscape: "Level Downs" and "umbrageous Grots and caves"; fountains, brooks, and lake; "Hill and Dale and Plain"; a profusion of flowers and groves of "rich Trees": nothing is missing. Great care is taken to ensure both variety of elements and harmony or congruency among them. A small instance: in many descriptions of the Garden there is a

unicorn, standing proudly, first among the animals; in Tin-
toretto's "Creation of the Animals," following God comes
the unicorn. Milton omits him. By this time he would have
lent a fabulous air to the scene, detracting from its convinc-
ing naturalness.

To return to spatial arrangements. Who looks out from the
vantage point of the Garden and what is to be seen? First we
are told that the verdurous wall of Paradise "to our general
Sire gave prospect large / Into his neather Empire neighbor-
ing round." (IV, 144–5) A little later this general panorama
becomes an axial vista down the valley of the Tigris-Euphra-
tes toward the Persian Gulf, but it is the reader, not Adam,
who looks when Milton points and sees how "*Eden* stretch'd
her Line / From *Auran* Eastward to the Royal Towrs / Of
Great Seleucia." (IV, 210–12) Similarly, on the other side,
when the sun sets in utmost longitude "beneath th' Azores,"
it is we who watch while Uriel glides back to his station. In-
terestingly enough, Gabriel, though posted in the gateway
on top of the eastern cliff, sees nothing. As a guard, he never
lets his gaze wander. Regarding Adam, the impression we
get is that he can look out if he wishes, either on the Mediter-
ranean or the Mesopotamian side, and is well aware of his
geographic situation. For that matter, he knows that the
earth is a globe; the heavenly bodies, he tells Eve, minister
light from land to land when she is asleep. Adam, neverthe-
less, is never seen looking over Gabriel's shoulder into his
own potential domain; he is, in Wordsworth's phrase, "true
to the kindred points of heaven and home." Though pro-
tected, he is not immured. His initial and enduring sense of
the Garden was of "A woodie Mountain; whose high top
was plaine, / A circuit wide, enclos'd, with goodliest Trees /
Planted, with Walks and Bowers." (VIII, 303–5) And this is
our own sense of it. Though we view it through the eyes of
God the Son, Raphael, Uriel, Gabriel, Michael, Adam, Eve,
Satan, and Milton, we cannot draw its lines. We finally agree
to see it variously. And although it offers vistas into the

great world, our gaze returns to and remains among its manifold delights.

The domestic architecture of Adam and Eve is nicely handled. There are strong tactile apprehensions. The bower is roofed with laurel and myrtle and above that "what higher grew / Of firm and fragrant leaf." (IV, 694–5) The walls are verdant, fenced up with odorous bushy shrubs and with acanthus; a mosaic of iris, roses, and jessamin fills in between. "Acanthus" suggests carved marble and "mosaic" reinforces the texture. Similarly, as we find violet, crocus, and hyacinth underfoot, we are saved from the deliquescent effect of an April garden by the phrase, "with rich inlay Broiderd the ground, more colour'd than with stone of costliest Emblem" (IV, 700–2) and we tread as firmly as on the elaborate inlaid paving of the churches Milton visited in Rome. The flowers and sweet-smelling herbs with which "Espoused *Eve* deckt first her nuptial Bed" (IV, 708–10) are not specified; Milton leaves this to Eve, as her private affair. But when she and Adam fall asleep, with gentle solicitude he throws over them a light coverlet: "These lulld by Nightingales imbraceing slept, / And on thir naked limbs the flourie roof / Showrd Roses, which the Morn repair'd." (IV, 771–3)

The meal which Raphael shares with Adam and Eve is served on a square, raised table of grassy turf, fit ground for the abundance of fruit which Eve produces. She is not deprived of her role as the archetype of housewives; she selects and presents in ordered courses her fruit, so that appetite is upheld with kindliest change; she prepares drink from grapes and berries; she has even the means, we are told, to store whatever will improve by keeping. While the table is of turf, the seats are covered with moss, a nice tactile differentiation, in view of what is not being worn. While the trio are sitting there, we might spare a moment to notice what Raphael is wearing. It is Milton himself who leads us in this way, variously, from one thing to another.

One of the commonplaces of criticism is that Milton calls our attention, with design, to the nakedness of Adam and Eve. The body is good; matter is good: why should not humanity in its perfection appear *nudus et nuda*? But let us observe also how desirable and how difficult it is to accommodate other elements to this central fact. How finely balanced this problem is we notice when Manet, though he follows Giorgione's "Pastoral Concert," does not quite manage to reconcile his one female and two male figures on the grass. When Raphael comes down to speak with the human pair, will he too come in celestial candour of being, also naked and, if not, what garment will he wear? You know the answer. He wore six wings and the footnote refers us to Isaiah 6:2, some words we heard confusedly in Sunday-school at a time when "twain" suggested only Huckleberry Finn: "With twain did he cover his face, with twain did he cover his feet, and with twain did he fly." But let us see how Milton rearranges this abundance of plumage. (v, 277–84)

> six wings he wore, to shade
> His lineaments Divine; the pair that clad
> Each shoulder broad, came mantling o're his brest
> With regal Ornament; the middle pair
> Girt like a Starrie Zone his waste, and round
> Skirted his loines and thighes with downie Gold
> And colors dipt in Heav'n; the third his feet
> Shaddowd from either heele with featherd maile ...

He is clothed in four enveloping pinions providing an upper and lower draping, while the final pair resembles those on Mercury's clean pair of heels. "Like Maia's son he stood." It is a difficult problem, which Milton solves with skill. Even Blake is reduced to showing Raphael in a long-sleeved garment, over which flows a suggestion of feathering.

In a reduced form, the same problem of the proprieties attends the guards at the gate. When on duty, they are armed and, as we can see in David's painting of the Romans and Sabines in battle, an armed man can be conceded as adequately costumed. When we first view them, however, by the great gate, we get the same effect as when we reach the Arc de Triomphe and find a stand of arms looming above our heads: "nigh at hand / Celestial Armorie, Shields, Helmes, and Speares / Hung high with Diamond flaming, and with Gold." (IV, 551–3) As we approach, we see that this unarmed "youth of Heaven" is engaged in heroic games; they are now antique Grecian athletes, like undraped youths upon a frieze.

Returning to the *fête champêtre* which Adam and Eve are sharing with Raphael, we might notice in passing that the human pair has more than one place for meals. The formal, square table is set for a heavenly guest, but earlier we have seen Adam and Eve reclining in the Etruscan or Roman manner on a "soft downie Bank damaskt with flours." (IV, 334) Here it is that the animals gather before them. To this place, where a soft, rich fabric seems to cover the couch, they customarily come, for here the animals expect them. What pastoral luxury is this. But let us return to larger spatial arrangements, to the largest of all, the open heavens.

The solar or starry heavens above the Garden are wholly benign, for the earth's axis has not yet shifted. Adam, not much concerned to look outward, looks up. The night sky is majestic, yet buoyantly cheerful, like Wordsworth's sky at the close of *The Prelude*: (IV, 605–9)

> *Hesperus* that led
> The starrie Host, rode brightest, till the Moon
> Rising in clouded Majestie, at length
> Apparent Queen unvaild her peerless light
> And o're the dark her Silver Mantle threw.

When night is past, the morning sky calls forth Adam's praise to God, as he reviews the wonders of celestial movements. Later on he has a long discussion of celestial mechanics with Raphael. My immediate point, however, is a simple one: Adam is fully aware that the archangel has, in his journey from heaven, moved through "distance inexpressible / By Numbers that have name" (VIII, 113–14), yet he himself, as man, neither sees nor conceives spatially anything beyond the stars. The enclosing hollow sphere that bounds our universe and its Parthenon-like aperture are beyond his ken. This is excellent. Adam suffers neither the terror of looking out into Chaos nor the claustrophobia of living within a shell. His sky is as marvellous as the sky in Addison's famous hymn; no less. It is completely credible because it is the sky we see at the vernal or the autumnal equinox.

Though Raphael concedes that the earth *may* revolve about the sun, Adam always finds himself directly under Heaven, the dwelling place of his Creator and Sustainer. His prayers never have to creep out from under, like a daffodil when the bulb is planted upside down or the prayers of New Zealanders when God looked only upon England. He and Eve are axially beneath Heaven's gate. The geocentric world which this implies is the world of our daily visual experience as we watch sunrise or sunset. Yet, without difficulty, we keep in the back of our minds the scientific heliocentric interpretation, and so do Raphael and Adam. Wittkower said of Bernini's cathedra in St. Peter's, "It is precisely the union of traditionally separate and even contradictory categories that contributes to its evocative quality." We may say the same here and for the Garden generally.

Milton is continually persuading and adjusting our vision so that Adam's world – the sum total within his range of perception – appears firmly structured and rationally bounded yet flexible, open to movement and, indeed, illimitable. We flow, circulate, shift position, persuaded by cross-references, by changing viewpoints, by similes that keep lightly tethering the Garden, in many filiations, to astronomy, geography, history, myth, legend, or common sense.

Within this beautiful space, what is the range of contact that Adam and Eve can experience? Who is there that they can talk to? Primarily and with vast happiness, of course, they talk to each other, he discursive and she intuitive. Any intrusion into their charmed circle would be a mistake. Raphael's single visit of some six consecutive hours is therefore managed with scrupulous care. His courtesy, his "affable" manner, his speech "as friend with friend" are all insisted on. Even so, the visit is a little more than Eve can take.

Before going on, we should spare a moment to pay tribute to Raphael's performance as an expositor and his ability to strengthen rather than break the charmed circle. Raphael's disquisitions establish the place of Eden in the cosmos, give it directional and moral polarity between heaven and hell, and, similarly, place it between past and future. Yet what he tells us does not have the immediacy of the passages which have introduced us to the Garden and shown us its inhabitants. By devices too complex to be discussed here, Milton gives to Raphael's accounts the brilliance, convincingness, and aesthetic distancing of a set of murals; for example, at the very beginning a word like "gonfalons" (v, 589) sets the tone. It belongs not to Adam's world but to a world of pageantry. Let us praise Raphael's ability to adduce massive sets of events remote in time and place from the Garden, to keep his great procession of events in a somewhat different plane of reality from the Garden, and still, at the close, to intensify the moral urgency of Adam and Eve's situation, not detract from it. Mark Twain once said he believed Shakespeare's plays were written by another man "of the same name." I am tempted to suggest that Raphael's pictorial and narrative skills are much the same as those of Raphael of Urbino. The mural decorations of the "stanze" of the Vatican present us with Biblical material, such as St.

Peter's deliverance from prison; mythological elements, such as Parnassus; and real or alleged events in Christendom, such as the coronation of Charlemagne and the baptism of Constantine. We are very much aware that some of these things could not have happened in the form of the record. It seems unlikely that Plato, Aristotle, Socrates, Alcibiades, Alexander, Epicurus, Pythagoras, Heraclitus, Diogenes, Euclid, Ptolemy, Zoroaster, and Raphael himself ever assembled in the School of Athens. Yet other walls are clearly historical and the total effect of the magnificent succession of apartments in this papal palace is to establish the legitimacy and responsibility of the pontiff, who is, in fact, *in situ*. Similarly, in the other Raphael's accounts, we take the War in Heaven to be a simulacrum of what occurred; we take the Creation as closer to actuality, for we know the world and its creatures; and we agree that the whole vast outrolling of informative, educative, and monitory material reinforces our belief in the actuality of the Garden, in the happiness and responsibility of its pair of lovers.

Having considered the very special case of Raphael, let us again ask, with whom do Adam and Eve normally converse? Adam's own story begins with a kind of syncopated infancy and childhood, which incidentally strengthens our identification with him. He, too, was in a state of "reaking moisture" (VIII, 256) and needed to be dried; he, too, learned to stand, walk, run, and speak. Then God appears to him, "of shape Divine." It is God the Father, for in a beautifully playful and intimate speech, which critics ought to balance off against His irritation in BOOK III, he refers to himself as "alone / From all Eternitie, for none I know / Second to me or like." (VIII, 405–7) But all this is, naturally, before Eve appears. It transpires, after the Fall, that Adam had been in the habit of conversing with the Son, the Second Person of the Trinity: "Where art thou, *Adam*, wont with joy to meet / My coming seen far off? I miss thee here." (X, 103–4) This situation is delicately handled. In their prelapsarian state of happiness,

Adam is never seen leaving Eve to go off and have a talk with God.

Apart from Raphael, we find that Adam and Eve have no conversation with the angels. Gabriel is never approached and, when Ithuriel and Zephon discover Satan squat like a toad at Eve's ear, they hale him off without waking the human pair. We feel the propriety of these avoidances. In a sense, the *donné* of the story would suffer, the rigour of the great moral experiment would be compromised, and our focus upon archetypal man and woman would be blurred if the presence of an angelic guard led to toing and froing, chatting, picnicking, and asking advice. Yet angels are, *ipso facto*, messengers. Some real rapport must be established. We get it in the deep concern of Gabriel and his subordinates for the safety of Adam and Eve. We get a suffused sense of it in the marvellous passage in BOOK IV, the full value of which is seldom elicited: (IV, 677–88)

> Millions of spiritual Creatures walk the Earth
> Unseen, both when we wake, and when we sleep:
> All these with ceaseless praise his works behold
> Both day and night: how often from the steep
> Of echoing Hill or Thicket have we heard
> Celestial voices to the midnight air,
> Sole, or responsive each to others note
> Singing thir great Creator: oft in bands
> While they keep watch, or nightly rounding walk
> With Heav'nly touch of instrumental sounds
> In full harmonic number joind, thir songs
> Divide the night, and lift our thoughts to Heaven.

In addition, Milton gives us just the smallest hint that Eve has some communication with angels on the subject of her gardening. She is furnished with "such Gardening Tools as Art yet rude, / Guiltless of fire had formd, or Angels brought." (IX, 391–2) As to what they might have brought: she reminds Milton, in lines immediately following, of Pomona, and Pomona, according to Ovid, carried a pruning hook. It adds to the goddess-like demeanour of Eve; it saves her from gardening with her hands; it is barely – in three words – brought to our attention.

The animals in the Garden keep exactly the proper distance from Adam and Eve. To Adam God had said: "know'st thou not / Thir language and thir wayes, they also know, / And reason not contemptibly; with these / Find pastime, and beare rule; thy Realm is large." (VIII, 372–5) Clearly this adumbrates the domestication of animals, but, like the adumbration of Eve's maternal rôle, it is fulfilled only after the expulsion. In the meantime, there are token performances: the ramping lion condescends to dandle the kid; the bear gambols; the elephant displays his strength and wreathes his lithe proboscis. It is very gay, very touching, very charming, and nothing is carried too far. Adam spends no time walking with the dog and Eve has no pets about the house. There is an exact propriety of distance.

Let us now move on to Milton's handling of time. The father of Edmund Gosse, you recall, was a naturalist and, in his reading of the Bible, a literalist. He encountered the problem, which can take many forms, as to whether the trees of the Garden had annual rings or whether, if cut across, they would have showed a consistency like marzipan. It is the problem of process, which involves time. We must not now get into this problem, on any account, but we should take note of Milton's skill in preventing its irruption into his story. The garden must grow and, indeed, we see trees that bear "Blossoms and Fruits at once of golden hue." (IV, 148) But how unerringly Milton has singled out the orange tree, which is a tree for all seasons. It is always Spring in the Garden and yet the advantages of seasonal change, such as ripening, are preserved, and the onset of Winter avoided. There is no trace of change and decay, of mutability and transience, of debility and death.

The freshness and bloom of Eden owe something to there

being no backlog of time to account for. As we enter, Adam and Eve have not yet told each other what they can remember, and when told it is very little. Their days are just beginning to succeed "in an uncumulative series" – to borrow a phrase from Robert Finch. One of the devices of Baroque is to produce precision in the midst of boundlessness and we see with precision how our reckoning of days began. Raphael's story of creation ends with the withdrawal of the heavenly hosts; the earth and air were resounding with music "While the bright Pomp ascended jubilant." Raphael looks at Adam and says, "Thou remember'st, for thou heardst." (VII, 561–4) The gears shift quietly and our kind of time is begun.

This series of Adam's days, so carefully started and as yet barely started, runs the risk of setting up in our minds the expectation of a biological cycle. We have seen how Milton avoids the horticultural annual round. With no less care he avoids the cycle of "birth, copulation and death" by a simple device of sublimation: "And from these corporal nutriments perhaps / Your bodies may at last turn all to Spirit / Improv'd by tract of time, and wingd ascend / Ethereal, as wee, or may at choice / Here or in Heav'nly Paradises dwell." (V, 496–500) The children of Adam and Eve may spread into Eden and the whole Earth or climb to paradises above. No one need die.

It is hard to tear oneself away from that banquet, where Raphael has talked with such persuasive eloquence and where every word of Milton's description has flowered into new meanings – "pure," applied to Eve's kitchenware, avoids the barbarity of coconut shells, evokes the holiness and scrupulousness of Jewish ritual, and gets out of washing up. But it is time to refer, briefly and in closing, to a few large overall considerations making for the happiness of Adam and Eve. There are, for example, two benign paradoxes which run parallel to one another.

Baroque grandeur and firmness of structure, Baroque

logic and pervasive power, are everywhere apparent. (IV, 776–9)

> Now had night measur'd with her shaddowie Cone
> Half way up Hill this vast Sublunar Vault,
> And from thir Ivorie Port the Cherubim
> Forth issuing at th' accustom'd hour stood armd
> To thir night watches ...

Against this precision and resonance Milton deploys a ceaseless rippling flow of changing shades of light, of running water (the river does not lead out of the Garden, but plays within its borders), and of perfumes delicately profuse and pervasive: "As when to them who saile / Beyond the *Cape of Hope* and now are past / *Mozambic*, off at Sea North-East windes blow / *Sabean* Odours from the spicie shoare / Of Araby the blest." (IV, 159–63)

Parallel to this fruitful opposition, we find another which enriches the relation of Adam and Eve. The magnificent world in which they live has its psychological counterpart. They already have, in fact, a paradise within them. The external beauty and splendor of the Garden have a correlative within the mind, without which they would be meaningless. We can take this thought on many levels, beginning with Eve's lyric cry that, without Adam, this delightful land, with herb, fruit, flower glistering with dew and fragrant after showers, means nothing to her, and Adam's reciprocal anticipation that without Eve the Garden would be nothing but "wilde Woods forlorn." (IX, 910) We can take it from there as far as we like, until perhaps all *Paradise Lost* becomes the story of one's own inner and secret life. If Adam and Eve live supremely in our own hearts, the happier we, the happier they.

But even as we twitch our mantle and prepare to leave the Garden, yet carry it within us, the mind is haunted by the unbelievable richness of Milton's text, reaching out phrase by phrase to hold and keep us. The very blanks are filled with significance. There is, for example, no fire in the Garden; it is an alien element; everything Adam and Eve contrive must be "guiltless of fire." There is fire enough in Hell, we know, and it was preceded and adumbrated by Satan's forming and firing of artillery in Heaven. Fallen Adam will discover fire in the refracted rays of the sun or in the kindling by lightning of gummy bark of fir or pine. Tubal-Cain can use fire and may get the metal for his first tools from ore casually melted by forest fire. Satan reminds the reader of Prometheus but the analogy is never developed. There is "pernicious" fire in Heaven, directed against the rebel angels. To complete the scale we need gracious and beneficent fire in Heaven, and in BOOK XI it appears in the Golden Altar and Golden Censer filled with incense through which the Son presents the prayers of the saints to the Father. The pastoral innocence of the Garden, where no fire is needed or can come, is thus a happiness intensified and thrown into relief by these many, varied kinds of flame within the poem.

Milton's Garden offers us the image of permanent happiness, of bliss undiminishing and undiminishable. It is customary to sneer a little at the concept, to hold that the human condition demands continuous change and to imply that Milton was himself subconsciously on the side of rebellion and upheaval. It is an easy assumption that existence in the Garden, like worship offered by angels in Heaven, would in the long run become monotonous. I have tried to suggest that we are not obliged to take this view.

If it is argued that, even in Milton's scheme of things, the Garden is unique and transitory, its stability no more than a springboard to project Adam into the future, we might still remember that, in the tumultuous world of human history, Adam is promised the possibility, through faith, of a paradise within, happier far, from which he cannot fall. We might also recall that history itself will end and "then the Earth / Shall all be Paradise, far happier place / Then this of *Eden*, and far happier daies." (XII, 463–5)

It will be said that this is outside human experience and therefore of no value to us. On the contrary, this is the world to which the vision of Dante, of Raphael, of Bach (if, for a moment, I may use the great names casually) leads us. Even our contemporary concepts of time, space, and the cosmos point toward a transcendence of historical sequence as we experience it.

We may return to the Garden, then, and to its peculiar quality of "secure delight" – to use *L'Allegro*'s phrase – with the confidence that we are not dealing with a pastiche of old illusions or a half unwilling compliance with some sterile orthodoxy, but rather with an image of abundant joy and vitality "which God hath prepared for them that love him."

THE REVELATION TO EVE

NORTHROP FRYE

$\mathfrak{D}$reams are of great importance in the Classical epics, where they may be true or deceitful, and may descend through the gate of ivory or of horn. An epic designed to justify the ways of God to men would have to be especially careful in its treatment of dreams: in Homer Zeus himself may send a deceiving dream as well as a true one, but in *Paradise Lost* the two gates must be as wide apart as the gates of heaven and hell themselves.

The creation of Adam is associated with two dreams: first a dream of the trees of Paradise, then a dream of Eve. In both cases Adam awakes to find the dream true. Keats was later to see in these dreams a symbol of the imagination of the poet, which tries to realize a world that others can understand and live in, and is therefore a fully creative and not merely a subjective or fantastic power. Milton's meaning is different but not wholly dissimilar. Adam's dreams are prompted by appetite in its two main forms of food and sexual love. In the unfallen state appetite is good, being a part of God's creation, and what Adam calls "mimic Fancy" is aligned with reason. What Adam wants, in short, is what Adam has: desire in the unfallen state is completely satisfied by the appropriate object. Eve's dreams, like Adam's, are very close to her waking experience, and help to bind together her sense of time in a world too happy to have much history: "Works of day pass't, or morrows next designe." (v, 33) The Satan-inspired dream of Eve, on the other hand, uses the kind of symbolism that we now think of as typical of a dream. Because she is unfallen, such a dream can only come from outside her, though, like Bunyan's Christian in the Valley of the Shadow, she is troubled to think that it may have proceeded from her own mind. She is right by anticipation: since the fall, inner desires which are excessive by nature and can never be satisfied have taken root in us, and produce the wish-fulfilment fantasies of lust and greed, which are the two appetites in their fallen form. They are the reflection in us of what Satan describes as (IV, 509–11)

> fierce desire,
> Among our other torments not the least.
> Still unfulfilld.

After the fall, Adam, fully awake and conscious, receives from Michael his second revelation, the tremendous Biblical vision of the future, stretching from Cain to the Last Judgment, with which the great poem reaches its close. From the previous revelation of Raphael Eve had absented herself, in order to hear it later from Adam alone. But now Adam is less trustworthy as a medium of revelation: while he wakes to hear the revelation, Eve is put to sleep, as Adam was when she was created, the little symmetry in the design being called to our attention. (XI, 369) Eve is given dreams which are inspired this time by God instead of by Satan, and which constitute a revelation that is distinctively hers. We are told

very little about these dreams, except that their central sub-
ject is the defeat of the serpent by a redeemer descended
from her.

The famous, or notorious, line in *Paradise Lost* (IV, 299)
about the relations of Adam and Eve, "Hee for God only,
shee for God in him," illustrates a central problem in reading
the poem. This is the problem of the language of analogy.
The statement is made of the unfallen Adam and Eve, and so
is not literally true of men and women as we know them.
Fallen life shows an analogy to unfallen life, and the analogy
accounts for the social supremacy of men over women that
we find assumed in the Bible, from the account of the fall it-
self in *Genesis* (*Gen.* iii.16; *PL*, x, 195–6) to St. Paul's direc-
tives for the primitive Church. But obviously no fallen son of
Adam can represent God in the way that the unfallen Adam
could. The example of the unfallen Adam merely puts a
heavier responsibility on his male descendants to be worthy
of what ought to be a purely spiritual authority. Similarly,
monogamous marriage arises in the world as a fallen analogy
of the divinely sanctioned union of Adam and Eve, and a
prejudice in favour of the permanence of all marriages is
therefore justifiable. But, for Milton, to prohibit divorce alto-
gether is to ignore the fact that the relation of ordinary to
paradisal marriage is analogous only, and that the realities of
unfallen life are ideals, not always attainable ones, in this
world.

The analogy also extends in the other direction. The rela-
tion of man to woman symbolizes, or dramatizes, the relation
of creator to creature. God speaks of himself as male, and his
revelation uses the terms Father and Son, although in most
contexts, apart from the Incarnation, we can hardly ascribe
literal sex to the Deity. We think of God as male primarily
because he is the Creator: we think of Nature as female, not
merely as a mother from whose body we are born, but as a
creature of God. Human souls, including male souls, are
symbolically female when thought of as creatures: the re-

deemed souls of men and women, who are aware of their status as creatures, make up a female church or Bride of Christ. Among spirits, whether fallen or unfallen, sex is not functional: spirits can be of what sex they please (I, 423–4). But in human life the sexes represent the polarizing of man's existence between God and Nature, creation and creature. Man is set above woman to remind him of the rightful places that God and Nature respectively should hold in his life. Adam's substance, so to speak, is in the God who created him: in himself, apart from God, he is only the shadow of himself. Similarly Eve's substance is in Adam, as her formation from his rib indicates.

Being cut off or "alienated" (IX, 9) from God puts one into the state of pride. This state is subjective, and needs an object, which is normally an idol, idolatry being the worshipping of something created instead of the creator. For Adam, once turned away from God, the most immediate idol is the fallen Eve, the fairest of creatures, and for his descendants idolatry becomes a debased form of woman-worship, of taking woman, along with the Mother Nature to which in this context she belongs, to be numinous instead of a creation ranking below man on the chain of being. For Eve, on the other hand, the root of idolatry is self-worship. There is nothing wrong with her admiring her own image in the water, but the episode suggests, again by anticipation, the story of Narcissus, who fell in love with his image – that is, exchanged his real or divine self for his own subjective shadow. The direction of the fallen Narcissus is also Satan's, as his "daughter" Sin indicates when she says to him: (II, 764–5)

Thy self in me thy perfect image viewing,
Becam'st enamourd.

But the fact that man is capable of idolatry is connected with the peculiar role of sex in human life. The devils are not, strictly speaking, idolaters: they are atheists or fatalists.

They assert that they were not created by God, and origi-
nated directly from nature, but they have no occasion to
associate nature with anything feminine.

In Classical mythology there is a pervasive sexual symbo-
lism which points to a blurred memory on the part of fallen
man of the relation of God to his creation. The chief of the
gods in this mythology is a male sky-god, Jupiter, who,
where the context is appropriate, may be spoken of by a
Christian poet in terms recalling the Christian God without
violation of decorum. But the fact that Jupiter has a consort
who is also his sister – *et soror et coniunx*, as Virgil says –
shows that the original Jupiter is, like Juno, a deified spirit of
nature, not a creator qualitatively distinct from his creation.
Classical myth, vaguely aware that a spirit of nature, when
deified, is a devil, also said that his rule was an usurpation,
and that before him there was a golden age of Saturn and
Rhea, when, as Milton ingeniously suggests in *Il Penseroso*
(23–6), incestuous unions might have been innocent. The
myth of the golden age takes us one step nearer to the
authentic revelation of the original state of man. One very
brief passage in the *Argonautica* picked up by Milton (x,
580–4) hints that Saturn and Rhea in their turn succeeded
a still more primitive pair, Ophion and Eurynome. The word
Ophion, serpent, indicates that we here are very close to a
genuine memory of the real beginnings of idolatry. Eury-
nome means wide-ruling: Milton's gloss, "the wide- / en-
croaching Eve perhaps," is somewhat puzzling, but it seems
to say that the memory of the fallen Eve is the source, for the
heathen, of the myth of a great mother-goddess from whom
all deified principles in nature have ultimately descended,
even though their fathers are the fallen angels.

Classical mythology does not clearly separate creator and
creature, but it does contain a sexual symbolism which, as we
should expect, puts the male above and the female below.
Milton himself uses this symbolism in both Classical and
Christian contexts. The male principle in nature is associated

with the sky, the sun, the wind, or the rain. The specifically
female part of nature is the earth, and the imagery of caves,
labyrinths, and waters issuing from underground recall the
process of birth from a womb. Trees and shady spots gen-
erally, and more particularly flowers, are also feminine, and
so is the moon, the lowest heavenly body. The imagery of the
labyrinth or maze is associated sometimes with meandering
rivers, sometimes with a tangle of shrubs or trees. A forest so
dense that the (male) sky is shut out, as in the "branching
elm star-proof" of *Arcades*, may be a symbol of natural vir-
ginity, the abode of Diana. The sexual union of sun and
earth is celebrated with great exuberance and power in Mil-
ton's *Fifth Elegy*, on the coming of spring. In *Paradise Lost*
Adam smiles on Eve. (IV, 499–501)

> as Jupiter
> On *Juno* smiles, when he impregns the Clouds
> That shed *May* Flowers,

an allusion which places Jupiter and Juno definitely in the
category of deified nature-spirits. Similarly Adam's voice
calls to Eve "Milde, as when *Zephyrus* on *Flora* breathes."
(V, 16)

In Biblical symbolism, too, the earth or fertile land is often
in a feminine relation to its ruler or owner, representing
what Milton calls "the holy covenant of union and marriage
between the king and his realm," meaning in this context
Charles I, though he was later to ridicule the same king for
thinking of his parliament as "but a female." The land of
Israel is called "married" (Beulah) by Isaiah, and the "black
but comely" bride of the Song of Songs is also associated
with the fertile land ruled by King Solomon. When Adam
awakens Eve in BOOK V he addresses her in language pre-
figuring (or, for the reader, recalling) the aubade of the bride
in the Song of Songs. It is also the Song of Songs that intro-
duces the image of the female body as an enclosed garden
(*hortus conclusus*) which had an extensive religious and

poetic later life. We are not surprised to find the garden of Eden in *Paradise Lost* described in feminine imagery, with its river rising from underground and running "With mazie error under pendent shades" (IV, 239), and where a vine "gently creeps," in an image later associated with Eve's hair. The newly created Eve awakens "Under a shade [i.e. tree] of flours," and the first thing she sees is her own reflection in a lake "Of waters issu'd from a Cave." (IV, 450–4) The contrast with Adam awakening in the sunlight and inspecting first of all his own body is clearly deliberate.

The fallen forms of the two human appetites are lust and greed: in a more demonic context they become force and fraud, the two weapons of Satan. Satan finds that he is unable to destroy the world by force. God displays the scales, the symbol of created order, in a significant place in the sky, between the Virgin of divine justice and the scorpion, and Satan, then as later in *Paradise Regained* able to read the future in the "Starry Rubric" (*PR*, IV, 393), does not try to fight. The scales prefigure the later rainbow, which guarantees the permanence of the natural order after the deluge. Satan's only effective weapon, then, is fraud, and fraud creates an evil analogy to the good. The greatest good for Eve is knowledge of God through Adam: Satan presents her with a dream of attaining knowledge, and eventually godhead, for herself, under the image of suddenly rising from the earth into the air, where she is just as suddenly abandoned. The sexual sensations of flying and falling, and the orgasm rhythm of the whole dream, show that Satan's symbolism is as eloquent as his rhetoric. This demonic surge upward to the sky suggests two other images: the Gunpowder Plot and the struggles of rebellious Titans bound under exploding volcanoes, both of which enter the imagery of *Paradise Lost*. We have also the Limbo of Vanities, the upward sweep of those who try to take heaven by force or fraud. After the flood, when man settles down systematically to idolatry, a more solid image of demonic pride, the Tower of Babel, is set up.

Eve rises into the air, where she sees "The Earth outstretcht immense, a prospect wide." (v, 88) The air is, later, Satan's headquarters, as Satan appears to realize already ("in the air, as we," he says). From there, it is further suggested, she may rise to heaven if she likes, and see what the gods are doing. She seems to be symbolically at the point, usually represented by a mountain-top under the moon, which is the boundary between terrestrial and celestial worlds in Dante's *Purgatorio*, Spenser's *Mutabilitie Cantoes*, several poems of Yeats, and elsewhere, and would also have been the top of the Tower of Babel if that point had ever been reached. The imagery of Eve's dream of ascent is echoed in the later elevation of Adam, who is taken to a hill (XI, 378–80)

> Of Paradise the highest, from whose top
> The Hemisphere of Earth in cleerest ken
> Stretched out to amplest reach of prospect lay.

where Michael's vision is displayed to him. Eve at this time is placed on a much lower level to receive her dreams – another example of the curious antithetical symmetry which pervades the poem. The elevation of Adam in its turn is explicitly compared to Satan's placing of Christ on a mountain top during the temptation (though in *Paradise Regained* the climactic temptation was shifted to the pinnacle of the temple, following Luke's order). We can understand the link between Satan's temptation of Eve and his temptation of Christ, but why should God's purely benevolent design of imparting prophetic knowledge to Adam be included in the same complex of imagery?

The reason is that Satan is not the only one who can construct analogies. God constantly frustrates Satan by turning to good what Satan intended to be evil. Adam's new knowledge of good and evil, "That is to say, of knowing good by

evil," is placed in its proper context of the revelation of God
to man which is later recorded in the Bible. Even outside
Christianity the same principle operates. The word "fall" is
a spatial metaphor: we are now "down," and any effort to
better ourselves must take us "up." Leaving Christianity out
of account for the moment, there are both good and bad men
in the world; both wish to go "up," and both have to start
from the same point. The bad man recognizes no God except
what he considers to be his own good, and his life is a struc-
ture of pride like the Tower of Babel. The good man – let us
say a virtuous heathen – recognizes the existence of a good
that is not himself, and attempts to seek for it. One con-
spicuous result of such imaginative virtue is the structure of
Classical poetry and philosophy, a natural and reasonable
human analogy of revelation – not itself revelation, of
course, or possessing any final authority, but an impressive
monument, none the less, of the wisdom which still remains
implanted by God in the human mind. This structure is a
kind of virtuous Tower of Babel: there is a considerable con-
fusion of tongues in it, but it represents man dreaming of his
Creator, and following the impulse to return to his Creator
which is an original part of his nature. We may call it the
anabasis of Eros. Love awakes in the soul, is attracted first
by objects of sense, and then by more abstract and concep-
tual elements until it begins to draw nearer to God. Once
Christianity appears in the world, this analogical structure of
love is not abolished but becomes a supplement to its revela-
tion. As such it forms the basis for the imagery of a good
deal of Milton's own poetry, including the bulk of his earlier
poetry. A pedagogical version of it is the model for Milton's
ideal curriculum of education.

The lower part of this analogical structure is composed of
Classical mythology. Classical myths, the fables of the
heathen, are almost literally dreams, blurred and distorted
versions, created partly by memory and partly by fancy, of
what the Bible presents, in Milton's view, so much more

simply and plainly. They are dreams of man as a child of Eve
rather than of Adam, and are dominated by female images
and personalities. Mother Nature, and more particularly
Mother Earth, appear as the great *diva triformis*, the goddess
of the moon, the forest, and the lower world, all symbolically
female regions, or as Venus, the goddess of sexual love who
personates the "God" (x, 145) that Eve became to Adam at
the moment of his fall. Venus has two male figures subordi-
nated to her, Eros and Adonis, the gods of love and death,
the poles of Mother Nature's cycle. The Spenserian image of
the Gardens of Adonis, with Venus presiding over her
wounded lover, appears at the end of *Comus*, a kind of erotic
Pietà, as Venus with the infant God of Love is a kind of
erotic Nativity. The dying-god flowers, the anemone and the
hyacinth particularly, appear in the Latin elegies, and again
in *Naturam non pati senium*, as ornaments of the Earth.
Tammuz (Adonis) himself, in both the *Nativity Ode* and
Paradise Lost, is introduced as the object of a female cult.
The image of a mother hiding or shrouding a male child, as
the Earth hides the seeds of new life, is associated with the
Garden of Eden, with the references to Amalthea hiding her
"florid son" Dionysus, and to the Abyssinian princes in their
prison-Paradise. (IV, 275–80) The feminine images of laby-
rinth, cave, flowers, shade, thicket, and moonlit night
partake of the darkness, mystery, lost direction, and conceal-
ment characteristic of religions of nature without the day-
light of revelation.

It is within this shrouding and enclosing female Nature
that the imagination of the poet awakens. In *Ad patrem*
Milton speaks of his poetry as dreams in a secluded cave.
The poet at this stage is psychologically close to the lover,
and what he loves, at first, is simply the sensuous beauty and
delight of nature in general, like the narrator of the First and
Seventh Elegies admiring all the pretty girls he sees on the
streets. The minor poet may remain at this stage of uncom-
mitted, or temporarily committed, attraction, sporting with

Amaryllis in the shade or with the tangles of Neaera's hair –
again we notice the thematic feminine words "shade" and
"tangles." If the poet-lover becomes more serious he may go
in either a right or a wrong direction. The wrong direction is
that of the courtly love convention of unquestioning obe-
dience to a mistress and the acceptance of the frustration
that her whims and coyness may cause. Milton shows a con-
sistent dislike of this convention and a reluctance to write
within it: for him it is the purest expression of "man's
effeminate slackness" (XI, 634) which allows a woman, and
hence the created nature which she represents, to have rule
over him. The right direction, of course, is marriage, the
wedded love which in *Paradise Lost* is contrasted with the
frustration of "the starved lover" and the jealousy which is
"the injured lover's hell." (IV, 769; V, 450) This is a rational
state in which the man is normally the superior, and its pro-
totype in Classical mythology is the union of love and the
soul represented by the Cupid and Psyche story in Apuleius.

It is conventional in courtly love poetry for the poet to
abandon sensuous love at a certain point and turn to ideal,
philosophical, or religious forms of love. Milton is unusual
however in the promptness with which he makes the break.
For him, as man continues to ascend the scale of his own na-
ture, the Adam within him awakes, and progressively domi-
nates the element of Eve. Man's attitude to the world around
him then becomes less sensuous and more rational. He be-
gins to think of nature less as a mother or mistress and more
as an intelligently designed and created order. Nature is
coming to represent less herself and more the wisdom of
God which the virtuous man is seeking. On the upper levels
of natural religion, one tends to become a Platonist, thinking
in terms of a lower world of the body and a higher world of
the soul, which may become released from the lower world
as from a prison. In Milton's earlier poems we meet flights in
the air which may be purely demonic like Eve's dream, as
notably in *In quintum Novembris*; or the symbolism may be
that of the soul escaping from the body and seeking its natu-

ral element in a higher world, as in the elegy on the Bishop
of Ely.

The lower part of the analogy of Eros is the world of
sense, where nature, the objective world, appears mainly in
feminine images to the perceiver. There are thus two levels
of nature, though there are also different ways of conceiving
these two levels. One way is that of the simple physical con-
trast of winter and summer. Nature in this context exists as
a cyclical movement between life and death. The earth rises
to pour out her treasures of life in the spring as the sun
awakens her, and sinks back to sleep in the winter. The
image of Proserpine, spending half the year below the
ground with her secret lover, and rising above the ground
for the other half, appears in *Paradise Lost* as a poignant
anticipation of Eve, driven from her natural habitat of Eden
to the cursed wilderness below. Arethusa, the nymph of the
underground river who rises with her lover Alpheus in
Proserpine's land of Sicily, is a similar image, appearing in
both *Arcades* and *Lycidas*. In the *Nativity Ode* Nature has
stopped her sexual activities partly out of respect for her
Creator and partly because it is too cold, or rather because
the sun is, and reposes in a sterility which assumes inno-
cence.

These two levels of nature modulate into a more concep-
tual relation in *Paradise Lost* as a lower level of chaos or the
abyss, "The womb of Nature, and perhaps her grave" (II,
911), and an upper level of cosmos or creation proper,
which comes into being after the abyss has been made preg-
nant by a male Spirit of God, who in natural imagery would
be associated with birds or the wind. The difference in this
perception of the two levels of nature is connected with the
difference between two views of death. Sensibly and objec-
tively, death is annihilation, a return to the underworld of
chaos; rationally, it is the separation from the sensible body
that enables one's immortal soul to live in the world appro-
priate to it.

As we rise to a still more penetrating vision of nature, its two levels take on the Platonic aspect just mentioned. Here we have a lower physical and sensible aspect and a higher intellectual one: nature as attractive object and nature as designed object or creature. The imagery of these two levels might be called the "allegro" and the "penseroso" imagery. The former is that of the earthly Paradise, as expressed in the fables of the Elysian fields and the gardens of the Hesperides; the latter is that of the music of the spheres, the sense of harmonious design that conveys to us the intuition that nature is not just there, as a mother is just there to a small child, but has been intelligently and purposefully put there by a power superior to her.

The poet in nature is thus placed in a far more comprehensive situation than singing the praises of pretty girls would ever reveal to him. Even in his most sensuous poetry, the poet feels links drawing him, not merely to nature, but to the hidden powers of nature, to whatever it is that can "keep unsteady nature to her law," in the words of *Arcades*. In the poem to Salzilli, Milton speaks of the poet's song as having the power to prevent floods: this is the image of the poet as a benevolent magician controlling nature by the "sweet compulsion" of his song, of which the archetype is Orpheus. This image frequently appears in Shakespeare, especially in *A Midsummer Night's Dream* and *The Tempest*, which one suspects were the favourite plays of L'Allegro. In these two comedies, the spirits of the elements represent powers of nature which are linked to human activity. Milton does not, like the later Romantics, make much of the metaphor of the poet as "creator," participating in the creative activity of God by producing poems, but he could certainly have understood what Coleridge meant by calling the poet a tamer of chaos. The poet identifies himself with the created order, with the law of unsteady nature against the annihilation into which by herself nature would plunge. The Salzilli image, with its affinities to magic and the figure of Orpheus, is thus connected with the imagery of the permanence of the created order which was reaffirmed after the flood, and confirmed by the emblem of the rainbow.

The poet, if he is following rightly his innate impulse to rise from nature to God, will not look in nature for anything numinous: the so-called gods of nature are devils. The elemental spirit, like Shakespeare's Puck or Ariel, is a more accurate image because such a spirit is, even when mischievous or unwilling, amenable to rational control. The Christian poet finds his identity with nature, not by looking for gods in it, but through a feeling of protection and security in nature which is ultimately a sense of the providence of God as revealed through nature. The symbol of this hidden beneficent design is the Genius, whether of the wood, as in *Arcades*, or of the shore, as in *Lycidas*. The Attendant Spirit and Sabrina in *Comus* are elemental spirits who take on this role of good Genius or guiding daemon in the lower world. The image of the Genius is Virgilian, but Milton indicates a larger background for it in the *Apology for Smectymnuus* when he speaks of "having read of heathen Philosophers, some to have taught, that whosoever would but use his eare to listen, might hear the voice of his guiding *Genius* ever before him, calling, and as it were pointing to that way which is his part to follow." (*Prose Works* I, 904) The Lady's "Echo" song in *Comus* helps to bring out this identity of human and physical nature as common creatures of God.

The poet's art is a musical one, in the Platonic sense: verse is closely allied to voice, and poems are generally described in musical metaphors as sung or played on a reed. The music that we know is a subordinate art to the verbal music of poetry, as Milton indicates in a parenthesis in *Paradise Lost*: "For Eloquence the Soul, Song charms the Sense." (II, 556) The curious context of this remark – he is speaking of the arts of the devils in hell – reminds us that the analogy of Eros is, outside Christianity, pervaded by demonic inspiration, and rooted in it. The greater human art is, however, the more obviously it becomes the praise of God, and as praise of God it forms a part of the response to the Creator by the creature which is what is meant, symbolically, by "harmony." Harmony includes both the music of the spheres in nature and "That undisturbed song of pure consent" in heaven referred to in *At a Solemn Music.*

As the poet gains in the understanding of the meaning of his own art, he realizes that his art is on the side, not merely of order as against chaos, but of life as against death. The supreme effort of Orpheus as poet was not to charm the trees, but to raise Eurydice from the lower world, his failure representing the inadequacy of unaided human art. (cf. III, 17 ff.) Prospero in Shakespeare claims that his magic was able to raise the dead, and the poet's music is at least "consent" with a life-giving power: "Dead things with inbreathed sense able to pierce." The metaphors here extend into medicine: in the Shakespearean romance of *Pericles* a doctor raises the dead (or what amounts to that) by music, and Asclepius as well as Orpheus haunts Milton's Latin elegies (especially, of course, the one on the death of the Vice-Chancellor, who was a doctor). In the *Apology for Smectymnuus,* again, Milton speaks of what Comus carries in his glass as "a thick intoxicating potion, which a certain Sorceresse, the abuser of loves name, carries about." (*Prose Works,* I, 892) The antidote for this, a healing drug or herb which leads one to knowledge and virtue, is mentioned in the *Second Elegy* and enters *Comus* as the mysterious "haemony," which is compared to the Homeric moly. The Biblical archetypes of the narcotic potion and haemony are of course the fruits of the trees of knowledge and life respectively.

If we may associate the Attendant Spirit with the musician Henry Lawes, it may be reasonable to associate his shepherd friend with the poet Milton, and see in this haemony something closely connected with the poet's art. Haemony is a dark inconspicuous plant which bears a flower in "another country" (*Comus* 630-2), and in *Lycidas* the image of a plant that does not grow here but bears its flower in another world is associated specifically with the poet's desire for fame. It is explained in *Lycidas* that fame, the love of which is an impetus powerful enough to make a poet "scorn delights and live laborious days," has nothing to do with Virgil's *fama* or rumour, but is a secular counterpart of what in Christian revelation is the hope of immortality. In *Paradise Lost* this image of the exotic flower appears as the amaranth (III, 353), which represents the genuine form of immortality, and originally bloomed beside the Tree of Life.

In writing within the analogy of Eros, the poet is elaborating and articulating a dream of man which is neither the dream that Satan gave Eve, nor the dream that God gave her later, but something in between: a dream about God based on the fallen knowledge of good and evil, in which, though the knowledge of evil may be primary, there is a great deal of good, and in the good a great deal of genuine pleasure. The pleasure is at its most eloquent, of course, in *L'Allegro* and *Il Penseroso*. The tone of *L'Allegro* is pastoral, the pastoral being the expression of the heightened pleasure that comes from simplifying one's wants and moderating one's desires, so that lust and greed subside into something more like their proper forms, "unreprovèd pleasures free." As night falls we encounter an expected series of images: elemental spirits recalling Puck and Queen Mab; Hymen, the spirit of wedded love; an erotic (Lydian) music expressly described as a maze or labyrinth, and finally an Elysian paradisal world. This is a world of (129–30)

Such sights as youthful Poets dream
On Summer eeves by haunted stream.

The word "haunted," in a context like this, has usually in it a sense of the gentler presences that impel us to associate Nature with feminine pronouns.

The imagery of *Il Penseroso* is even more explicitly feminine, from the "secret shades" where the goddess of Melancholy is born, to the moon wandering in the maze of the sky.

Here also the poet is a Platonist, speculating about the world inhabited by the soul when freed from the body, and about the spirits (95–6)

> Whose power hath a true consent
> With Planet or with Element.

"Consent" is again the musical metaphor, linked to the music sent by the "Genius of the wood" to the poet hiding from "day's garish eye" and sleeping in the lap of nature. The analogy of Eros stretches (at least in the poetic convention assumed) far back beyond Plato to the ancient teaching of the "thrice great Hermes," and continues through the magical imagery of mediaeval and Renaissance romance – the modern reader can see it continuing in Shelley and Yeats. Religious images also form a part of the "penseroso" dream: we notice, first, that they are images of "high church" practice – cloisters, stained glass, organ music, Gothic architecture – and, secondly, that they are appreciated on purely aesthetic grounds. The Nonconformist poet sees these tendencies in Christianity as a part of the analogy of Eros, to be enjoyed and appreciated in some contexts and condemned in others. Melancholy herself is a nun, not a Christian nun, of course, but a vestal virgin, being a daughter of Vesta.

Both she and Mirth take their poet to the upper limits of their dreaming analogy world. Mirth leads him to the earthly Paradise, an Elysium where Orpheus lies dreaming, and where he might be awakened, by the music the poet hears, to complete the redemption of Eurydice. The poem of melancholy, mentioning Orpheus in passing, leads to a hermitage where the poet learns the secrets of the inner harmony of nature, and comes "To something like Prophetic strain" (174) – that is, to an aesthetic analogy of religious experience. In these poems we are in substantially the same cosmos that the poet outlines in the *Vacation Exercise* poem, where in language oddly anticipating Eve's first dream, he can "look in" to the world of the gods, and comes to rest in the palace of Alcinous, whose gardens are another type of the earthly Paradise, and where music or poetry once again is an erotic maze of "willing chains and sweet captivitie." (35–52)

Of course one does not move upward effortlessly in this ascent of Eros. Every man, within Christianity or outside it, is faced in the world with a moral challenge. He cannot simply live on the unmoral level of plants and animals: he must either go downwards to sin or upwards to virtue. Mother Nature must ultimately become either the evil enchantress Circe or Hecate, or turn into some kind of *ewig-weibliche* inspiration like the Muse Urania or the Queen in *Arcades*. The first line of defence against Circe is reason, for the alliance of nature and reason is the key to the fact that Nature is a designed order, a fellow-creature of God. As Milton says, "they express nature best, who in their lives least wander from her safe leading, which may be called regenerate reason." (*Prose Works*, 1, 874) But reason in this world is a limited monarchy, and the great leap from the sensible to the intellectual world can result only from a moral revolution in the soul. Just as Eden was the home of man only as long as man remained unfallen, so nature in its purity, as the order God created and saw to be good, is perceptible only to the pure, the perception being symbolized by hearing the music of the spheres. Hence a need for purity in the major poet, a principle with an obvious personal application to Milton himself, which anyone but Milton might have found embarrassing. Even in that very light-hearted poem the *First Elegy*, there is a reference to the moly which may preserve the young poet from the enchantments of Circe, and in the Sixth Elegy there is a much more solemn statement of the contrast between the poet who remains on the sensuous level, celebrating wine and women in his song, and the poet who becomes what is described, still in Classical imagery, as the augur or priest of the gods. For the latter a rigid chastity is prescribed – chastity less as a virtue than as a necessary kind of discipline, like an athlete's training. We see that the impulse we have called Eros can develop away from the love of the sensuous toward the love of God so that nothing of the sexually "erotic" is left in it. This is not a paradox to any student of Plato, as Milton well understood, though Milton's fullest exposition of Plato's Eros, in *The Doctrine and Discipline of Divorce*, applies it mainly to wedded love.

The Lady in *Comus* has reached the pinnacle of the ascent of Eros, and has gone as far as natural virtue can go. Her chastity is virginity as well – an identification which is traditional in magic and romance, but in Milton indicates the non-Christian setting of the imagery. In an explicitly Christian poem chastity would not exclude marriage. In any case the Lady's chastity draws her away from the sensible world toward the world of the angels, who (456–62)

> in cleer dream, and solemn vision
> Tell her of things that no gross ear can hear,
> Till oft convers with heav'nly habitants
> Begin to cast a beam on th' outward shape,
> The unpolluted temple of the mind,
> And turns it by degrees to the souls essence,
> Till all be made immortal.

Immortality here is spoken of in Platonic terms as natural, the essence of the soul as distinct from the mortal body. Such a conception of it is, for Milton, not actually Christian but part of the "divine philosophy" of the brothers, which has hermetic, Platonic, and Neoplatonic affinities. Of course Milton in *Comus* is dealing with the conventions of poetry, not with the doctrines of religion or the facts of life, but even so the upper levels of virtue are not reached by the Lady entirely through her own efforts, hence the providential guidance given her by the Attendant Spirit. The further up one goes toward one's Creator, the more clearly the demonic element in Nature, its pollution by Sin and Death, becomes revealed. We are no longer, in *Comus*, within the world of

"unreprovèd pleasures free," where Bacchus has begotten
Mirth on Venus, but in a world of "grots and caverns
shagged with horrid shades," where Bacchus has begotten
Comus on Circe. The feminine images of darkness, the
forest, the labyrinth, the moon, the charm, the entanglement,
are here all connected with Hecate and Circe and the kind of
sensual degradation symbolized by Circe's beasts and the
sexual emblems borne by Comus, the enchanting rod and the
cup or glass.

The conflict in *Comus* is, like all of Milton's temptations,
a dialectical one in which the genuine and perverted versions
of the same ideas are separated. Comus and his followers
claim to "imitate the starry quire," and therefore among
other things to represent the genuine design of nature. The
Lady is tempted by the suggestion that innocence is both
amoral and natural, as the sex life of animals proves. The
Lady's resistance separates the humanly natural and inno-
cent from its opposite. There is a structural parallel with *The
Tempest*, where Prospero creates a humanly natural society
out of what is thrown on his island. His agent is Ariel, a
spirit natural but not human: there is no place for Ariel in
the new society, and he has to be set free in his own element.
The Lady has, without realizing it, been making use of the
Attendant Spirit, an elemental spirit of the upper air, as her
protector, and when she is freed, the Attendant Spirit, like
Ariel, returns to his own world. That world is nature in its
pure or original form, symbolized, not by the "penseroso"
heavenly spheres to which the Lady is attuned, but by the
"allegro" earthly-Paradise figures of Cupid and Psyche, their
offspring Youth and Joy, and the Gardens of Adonis. Again,
it is a central point in Milton's ethic that when man has done
all he can, God accepts what he does and strengthens man's
power. After Jesus has, *quasi homo*, done all he can, God's
power enables him miraculously to stand on the pinnacle of
the temple: after Samson has done all he can, God's power
takes over his will and sends him to the Philistine temple for

his triumphant martyrdom. Sabrina represents a similar extra power granted to the Lady, and the poem closes with the inevitably accurate lines: (1021–2)

> Or, if Vertue feeble were,
> Heav'n it self would stoop to her.

An explicitly Christian poem, like the *Nativity Ode*, would naturally have a different direction of imagery. The *Nativity Ode* deals, not with the anabasis of Eros, but with the katabasis of Agape, with the descent of divine love to man. Consequently, the images of *Comus* appear in roughly the reverse order. First comes the music of the spheres, in counterpoint to the song of the angels, unconscious and explicit praises of God respectively, then a vision of Nature in her original creation before the fall. The true gods, that is, the angels and the personified virtues, are a part of this vision, as is the reference to the "age of gold." Astraea, the goddess of justice, returns to the earth "Orbed in a rainbow," the rainbow, like the scales which are also an emblem of justice, being a recurrent image of the permanence in the order of nature. Fallen nature is now, of course, full of false gods, most of whom traditionally assume male forms. But we notice feminine imagery reappearing whenever there is any feeling of regret or nostalgia for the passing of the older order. Nobody regrets the passing of Moloch, but we feel differently about the nymphs who "in twilight shade of tangled thickets mourn" (the two thematic words again), about the Genius driven out of "haunted spring and dale," about the fairies obliged to leave, in the last phrase associated with the gods and spirits of nature, their "moon-loved maze." Finally we reach the Mother and Son in their genuine Christian ("Agape") forms, while the feminine "youngest teemed star" has overtones partly of Psyche, the bride of Eros, and partly of the wise virgins of the Bridegroom's wedding. Here as elsewhere we notice how the fact that Milton is unaccustomed to the word "its" (although it does

occur once in this poem), and substitutes "his" or "her" in-
stead, gives grammatical gender, and hence a trace of sexual
feeling, to the imagery. Thus hell is referred to as "her,"
which perhaps indicates that hell is to Satan what the Church
is to Christ, the society he leads and the environment he
lives in.

It is obvious that in Milton, as in most Christian poets,
the same images can be used in innocent or demonic con-
texts, and that the tone depends a good deal on whether the
theme is implicitly or explicitly Christian. We have already
met this principle in *Il Penseroso* and in the Genius, who may
be part of the apotheosis of Lycidas or part of the retinue of
false gods in the *Nativity Ode*. The fairy world, again, sug-
gests the free play of the imagination in *L'Allegro* and the
illusions of Satanic evil at the end of the first book of *Para-
dise Lost* and in *Comus*. Another Virgilian and magical
image of the enchantress charming the moon may be used
in a demonic context in *Paradise Lost*, where the labouring
moon eclipses at the night-hag's charms, or it may be used
playfully, in the context of the poetic Eros convention, as it
is in one of the Italian sonnets: (*Diodati, e te'l diro*)

E'l cantar che di mezzo l'hemispero
Traviar ben può la faticosa Luna.

In this context the image is an analogy of the conception of
harmony descending into chaos and forming a creation out
of it, so central to Milton's view of creation, the creation
being the primary example of what we have called the kata-
basis of Agape. It is also in connexion with a singer that
Milton makes a use, very rare for him, of this descending
Agape image in a secular context. The singer Leonora, it is
suggested, sings with the voice of the descending Spirit of
God, which pervades all things, and which teaches us
through her to become accustomed to the more rarefied
music of immortality.

Comus depicts the victory of innocence, and the help of

Sabrina shows that the Lady's innocence has been recognized by "Heaven." The analogy between Sabrina's sprinkling of the Lady and the rite of baptism, the introduction to revelation, is clear enough. *Paradise Regained* is a song of experience, beginning after baptism and recognition, and, in terms of the sexual symbolism, it is a man's vision of the powers behind nature, not a woman's dream of them. God made nature and is the real power behind it, but the visible part of nature, the part that corresponds to our dying bodies, has been usurped by Satan. Christ is, in our terms, the incarnation of Agape, to whom Satan exhibits the analogy of Eros as his domain. For the whole chain of being so far as we can see it, from chaos to man, and including the spirits of the elements, is Satan's, or so he claims: (*PR*, IV, 200–3)

> What both from Men and Angels I receive,
> Tetrarchs of fire, air, flood, and on the earth
> Nations besides from all the quarter'd winds,
> God of this world invok't, and world beneath.

The claim is considerably over-simplified, but it is true that the analogy of Eros is pervaded with a demonic element, and that it is Christ's task to recognize and reject that element. In *Paradise Regained* Christ descends, like Spenser's Guyon in the cave of Mammon, to a lower world, nature in its aspect as Satan's visible world displayed, where, unlike Proserpine, he refuses to eat so much as a pomegranate seed, rejecting every iota of it and making a complete break with it in order to ground himself wholly on the prophetic Hebrew tradition. Because he did this, we may say, speaking from Milton's point of view, the author of *L'Allegro* and *Il Penseroso* is able to be the most liberal and humane of poets, and the analogy of Eros is now safeguarded, not only by the providence of God, as in *Comus*, but by the Gospel as well.

We first enter the wilderness of Satan's kingdom, much

the same world as the demonic forest of *Comus*, being a "woody maze" and "A pathless Desert dusk with horrid shades," parts of it being also (*PR*, II, 296–7)

> to a Superstitious eye, the haunt
> Of Wood-Gods and Wood-Nymphs.

The suppression of explicit sexual imagery is connected with the fact that Satan realizes the uselessness of a sexual temptation of Jesus, as urged by Belial in a scrambled echo of the Song of Songs: (*PR*, II, 159–62)

> Virgin majesty with mild
> And sweet allay'd, yet terrible to approach,
> Skill'd to retire, and in retiring draw
> Hearts after them tangl'd in Amorous Nets.

Satan is always lying, even when talking to other devils or to himself, and his rejection of Belial's suggestion means that he is really adopting it, but in disguised and sublimated forms. His first major attack, after the failure of the first temptation, is on the two appetites, for food and for sexual experience. The emphasis is on food for obvious reasons, but the banquet he summons up is served by beautiful nymphs recalling the "faery damsels met in forest wide" of mediaeval romance. As Christ refuses one temptation after another, Satan is compelled to go further and further up the ladder of Eros, and in the temptations of Parthia and Rome he moves from passive to active sensuality. The forces of Parthia remind the poet again of the faery damsels of romance, specifically the Angelica of Boiardo and Ariosto, and the vision of the Emperor Tiberius hints at more elementary delights than purely administrative ones. Jesus' answer, with its echo of the "gold cup" of the Great Whore, who is the symbol of the persecuting Roman Emperors, indicates how clearly he sees the sexual cup of Comus in what Satan is offering: (*PR*, 116–19)

(For I have also heard, perhaps have read)
Their wines of *Setia, Cales,* and *Falerne,*
Chios and *Creet,* and how they quaff in Gold,
Crystal, and Myrrhine cups, embossed with Gems
And studs of Pearl.

Satan gradually realizes, with increasing contempt, that Jesus does not want the sublimated eroticism of power. What he must want, then, Satan assumes, is the kind of wisdom that Yeats calls the property of the dead, a wisdom involving a retreat from the world, or what we should now think of as a kind of return to the womb. Such a desire could be readily satisfied in the city which is under the patronage of the virgin goddess of wisdom: (*PR*, IV, 240–50)

Athens, the eye of *Greece,* Mother of Arts
And Eloquence, native to famous wits
Or hospitable, in her sweet recess,
City or Suburban, studious walks and shades;
See there the Olive Grove of *Academe,*
Plato's retirement, where the *Attic* bird
Trills her thick-warbl'd notes the summer long;
There, flowrie hill, *Hymettus,* with the sound
Of Bees industrious murmur, oft invites
To studious musing; there Ilissus rouls
His whispering stream.

The overtones of a shrouding female *hortus conclusus* are unmistakable, and the whole passage reads like a feeble parody of *Il Penseroso.* Satan, as usual, has the right explanation of Jesus' attitude in a perverted form. In the temptation, Jesus fulfils the law in the wilderness and becomes the true Joshua, or conqueror of the Promised Land, which is also the feminine garden of Eden. (*PR*, I, 7) In the Passion and Resurrection, Christ fulfils the prophecy made to Adam; by overcoming the temptation he fulfils the dream of Eve. The Virgin Mary, the "second Eve," is very prominent in the poem, and the typology of the whole temptation is summed up, from our present point of view, in the final line: "Home to his mother's house private returned."

We may notice in passing how Satan perverts even the genuine elements of the civilization he displays. What was really impressive about Greek culture, for Milton, was "the liberty of Greece" (*PL*, x, 307) that Xerxes tried to yoke. The philosophy of Plato and Socrates was a product of liberty, not, as Satan presents it, an escape from the world or a means of getting entangled in sophisticated arguments. "The Mountain Nymph, sweet Liberty," which appears in *L'Allegro* is certainly liberty in a different context, but it is not a wholly different kind of liberty. Satan's temptation of Athens ends "These rules will render thee a king complete," and Christ's answer ends "These only, with our Law, best form a king." Two conceptions of cyropedia, of education as the training of a prince, are colliding here. One leads to the conception of the king as a temporal ruler, who, if not a tyrant, would be the philosopher-king of Plato's "airy burgomasters," in Milton's phrase. The other is the institute of a Christian prince, leading to the king who is a spiritual ruler or prophet, a herald of freedom. A social and political aspect of Milton's analogical and sexual imagery is implied, and one which is set out in the prose works.

Jesus returns to his mother's house at the end of the temptation, but leaves it again to be about his father's business when he starts on his ministry, or work in the world proper. Here the female principle complementing Jesus is not the mother but the redeemed Bride or Church. Consequently it is semantically dangerous for Christians to think in terms of a Mother Church: it implies a regression to the law. "But mark, readers," says Milton, "the crafty scope of these prelates; they endeavour to impress deeply into weak and superstitious fancies the awful notion of a mother, that hereby they might cheat them into a blind and implicit obedience to whatsoever they shall decree or think fit." (*Prose Works*, I, 727–8) Christians should think of their

Church as a bride, a young virgin, still under tutelage. "For of any age or sex, most unfitly may a virgin be left to an uncertain and arbitrary education. ... In like manner the Church bearing the same resemblance, it were not reason to think she should be left destitute of that care which is as necessary and proper to her as instruction." (*Prose Works*, I, 755) This last means that the relation of Christ and the Church ought to be precisely the relation of Adam to Eve in the unfallen state. The conception is Pauline, but the interpretation of Paul involved is of course a left-wing Protestant one. The Word, the male principle, should have "absolute rule"; the Church has only to murmur "unargued I obey." The autonomous Church, who claims the authority to teach the Word herself, is in the position of the unfaithful bride or harlot identified with Israel and frequently denounced by the prophets, or else a man-made counterfeit of the Church, "Like that air-borne Helena in the fables."

Similarly society is in a female relationship to the prophet, the speaker of the Word, the possessor of Adam's spiritual authority. Delilah, like Job's wife, represents the threat of the forces of social inertia and habit to the voice of genuine leadership, or prophecy. There are two degrees of female recalcitrance in the Bible: there is Israel as the disobedient harlot of Hosea and Ezekiel, who is eventually forgiven and brought back to repentance, and who is represented in Christian tradition by the story of Mary Magdalene, and there is the Great Whore, the consolidated form of social apostasy, Delilah as Philistine. They correspond respectively to the fallen Eve and her demonic shadow in nature, the aspect of her that tempted Adam to fall too. Here we see the relevance of the theme of divorce in Milton to his sexual imagery. Milton's arguments for divorce do not concern us here; but behind these arguments is a larger symbolic structure in which the intolerable wife is the symbol of the custom and error that entangles the prophet. Adam could have

prevented his fall only by "divorcing" Eve after she had
fallen, and before Jesus can return to his mother's house he
has to complete a parallel divorce from the entire fallen
human society, which of course for Adam consisted only of
Eve. This divorce of Christ, being a recreation of man,
repeats the original creation, "when by his divorcing com-
mand the world first rose out of chaos, nor can be renewed
again out of confusion, but by the separating of unmeet
consorts." (*Prose Works*, II, 273)

A secular counterpart to the symbolism of Word and
Church also appears in the prose. Thus we read of "men
enchanted with the Circaean cup of servitude," and mazes
and labyrinths and coverts, whether of argument or of
action, often have a latent suggestion of some enchantress
hampering the freedom of a warfaring Christian. On the
other hand, Truth in the prose is often personified in terms
recalling the innocent and naked Eve. Truth and Justice, so
closely associated in the *Nativity Ode*, are explicitly identi-
fied in *Eikonoklastes*. Truth for Milton is existential, being
ultimately a person and not a principle or rational vision:
hence Truth is also the Astraea represented by the Virgin
of the zodiac, already mentioned, who is flanked with the
scales symbolizing justice within its context of God's
creative and ordering power. The vision of Truth in
Areopagitica and elsewhere is thus closely associated with
the insight into the harmony of created nature in *Comus* and
At a Solemn Music. Both aspects of Truth take us upward
to the Wisdom personified in the Bible as the daughter of the
Creator, playing before him when the world was ordered,
and the exact opposite of Athene, the virgin mother of
Athens whom Jesus has to abandon before he can return to
the home of the genuine virgin mother. If he had not
abandoned her, she would eventually have turned into Sin,
the daughter who was born of Satan much as Athene is said
to have been born of Zeus. Sin is described as serpentine,

like the Gorgon's head on Athene's shield: it seems strange that this image can represent a genuine ideal in the context of *Comus,* but so it is.

What we have been looking at in Milton's imagery is a particular way of relating the two great mythological structures on which the literature of our own Near Eastern and Western traditions has been founded. One structure is dominated by a male father-god, stresses the rational order of nature, and thinks of nature as an artefact, something designed and constructed. The other centres on a mother-goddess, perennially renewing the mystery of birth in the act of love. The father-god myth subordinates the female principle, making it a daughter-figure of Truth or Wisdom; the mother-goddess myth subordinates the male principle, making it the son-lover-victim figure of the dying god. The male mythology was dominant from the beginning of the Christian era down to the Romantic movement. In the mediaeval and Renaissance period its rival was incorporated in the Venus-Eros cult of the courtly love convention. After the Romantic movement began, the mother-centred myth gained ground. The father-myth is an inherently conservative one; the other is more naturally revolutionary, and the revolutionary emphasis in Milton shows how near he is to the mythology of Romanticism and its later by-products, the revolutionary erotic, Promethean, and Dionysian myths of Freud, Marx, and Nietzsche. The artefact myth has declined during the last two centuries partly because so many of its central elements came to be regarded as fictions, and again it is interesting to see how these elements in Milton are represented by symbols either known to be fictions, like the music of the spheres, or presented as possible fictions, like the Ptolemaic cosmos.

Milton of course accepted the artefact myth as primary along with the traditional ideas about how the sexual myth was to be subordinated to it. But he was also a poet who understood the claims of both on the imagination. The father-god myth has a moral principle built into it: it assumes a creator with an intelligent and purposeful Plan A for man's creation, who after Adam's defection falls back on an equally well designed Plan B for his salvation. The mother-goddess myth has only very ambiguous moral principles: it expresses an unconditioned desire which, either as that or in its frustrated form of resentment, may go in any direction and take any form. Theoretically, as we said, Eve's dream is fulfilled in the moment that Christ is raised, as she was, to a high eminence by Satan, then left to fall, and is sustained by the power of God as Satan falls instead. But Eve had shown, even in the unfallen state, a disconcerting capacity to have her own thoughts, her own desires, her own resentments even, to arrive at her own conclusions independently of Adam's superior reason. This tendency had led her to separate herself from Adam and fall under Satan's influence. God, who made her as she was, nevertheless had her separated again, and perhaps let her dream more or less in her own way: Michael suggests that he is only establishing the general atmosphere: (XII, 595–6)

Her also I with gentle Dreams have calm'd,
Portending good

and Eve's own account is even vaguer. It is significant that the revelation to Adam is so full and explicit, extending through most of two whole books, and the revelation to Eve so briefly, even evasively, referred to. The awakened father of mankind follows the master plan of God's salvation as it is unrolled scene by scene, and agrees to the justice, wisdom, and reason incorporated into it. We are expected to be similarly convicted and convinced, but, if the clear light of reason is ever dimmed by a passion or emotion that is not quite so sure of its objects, we may remember that, far below this rarefied pinnacle of rational vision, there lies a humiliated mother dreaming of the vengeance of her mighty son.

"PARADISE LOST"

The Relevance of Regeneration

ARTHUR E. BARKER

The accidental collocation of a literary tercentenary with a national centenary might, by its insignificant patness, serve only to confirm in their pessimism those who read *Paradise Lost* as a repudiation of ordinary human experience and find in its last books only a repudiation of history as the record of unrelievedly wilful human perversity. What could seem less appropriate to the commemoration of a creative act of confederation than the commemoration of the publication two hundred years before that of a poem which treats (I, 1–4),

> Of Mans First Disobedience, and the Fruit
> Of that Forbidden Tree, whose mortal tast
> Brought Death into the World, and all our woe,
> With loss of Eden ...,

a poem whose comment on history has been thought suffi-
ciently represented by the comment evoked from its poet
after his representation of the confederate agreement,
against man, of the fallen angels in Hell: (II, 496–505)

> Devil with Devil damn'd
> Firm concord holds, men onely disagree
> Of Creatures rational, though under hope
> Of heavenly Grace: and God proclaiming peace,
> Yet live in hatred, enmity, and strife
> Among themselves, and levie cruel warres,
> Wasting the Earth, each other to destroy:
> As if (which might induce us to accord)
> Man had not hellish foes anow besides,
> That day and night for his destruction waite?

One sort of answer to the querulous objection to merely
accidental collocation is perhaps contained in this last pas-
sage itself, with its reference to what may be confidently
hoped for and what Milton's God consistently proclaims.
And this sort of answer has been and will be variously
implied by the gifted Canadian scholars and critics who are
addressing us here. But their very presence here, and ours,
constitutes an answer whose force must be noted, since it
was undoubtedly the chief motive for those we must thank
for the creation of this occasion and for thus bringing us
together. It is but right that, among other assertions appro-
priate to 1967, there should be occasion for representing
the contribution of Canadians to international literary
scholarship and critical interpretation. This contribution is
not the least among the contributions in which it is right that
pride should be taken. And the Canadian contribution to
Milton scholarship and criticism is eminently representative
of the general Canadian contribution to humanistic educa-
tion and the responsibly cultivated life of the mind.

This assertion of the creatively representative character of
Canadian Milton studies may be made despite – and in a

sense because of – the very limited claims that can be made for Milton's general influence, or for the influence of his major poem on the three-hundredth anniversary of its publication, as compared with its reputation and influence on its hundredth and two-hundredth anniversaries. It must be admitted that Milton is nowadays far from being the people's poet he once was in some degree, for good or improper reasons. He is certainly not nowadays in any notable sense the poets' poet, as he was through much of the eighteenth and nineteenth centuries. He is very much the poet these days rather of scholars and academic critics. This occasion has its special appropriateness in that, for such reflections as these make all the more remarkable the proliferation and development of Milton studies and Milton criticism during the last thirty years or so. It may be said that, in their extent and intelligence and learning, labour, and industry, and because of the limits of Milton's popular reputation and influence just now, Milton studies and Milton criticism by no means inadequately represent the effort being made these days by humanistic literary scholarship, in relation to the responsibilities of humanistic education.

At the same time, I must confess that I often find myself wondering whether this efflorescence of academic and critical studies of Milton is not – in having no popular but at best an academically humanist base – in some degree symptomatic of an uneasily assertive state of mind in the literary humanities. This is a reflection that is for me underlined by the sort of rarefied mythopoeic mystique that is illustrated by many recent and admired interpretations of *Paradise Lost*. Is the efflorescence perhaps partly to be explained by the recognition that the kinds of problems presented by Milton's career, and especially the kinds of scholarly and critical problems to be met in the appraisal of his epic on the Fall of man and the loss of Eden, provide a comforting and inspiriting analogy with the kinds of problems – as to function, assertion, and consequence – that confront the literary humani-

ties in our universities and in their relation to a society which
finds the social sciences and the sciences more significantly
relevant and which, so far as it has literary interests at all,
prefers, to the old and dated and academic or classical, the
most recent, the ephemerally stimulating, the variously
existential, or the psychedelic and hallucinatory?

I hasten to assure you that I am not about to embark on a
heartening lament over the plight of the literary humanities.
And yet there may be something not uninstructive in the
possible relation between the present situation of the literary
humanities (and especially of English departments) and the
recent inclination, so variously and brilliantly exemplified,
to interpret *Paradise Lost* as a mythopoeic triumph over
adverse circumstances and a malign fatality, as a super-
humanly poetic response to an experience of frustration and
defeat, flung in the face of history and the unilluminated
many not fit to be of its audience, in which "a world of woe,/
Sinne and her shadow Death, and Miserie / Deaths Har-
binger" (IX, 11–13), is transcended by inspired vision.

Our humanism has always, of course, set itself against
mere pedantry, outworn systems, and especially a mecha-
nized materialism. More persuasive and learned Canadian,
or originally Canadian, voices have so eminently exemplified
that, that there is no need for lame repetition here. But both
historical and present experience may lead us to reflect that,
when pedantry and systems become the tools of essentially
materialistic values, humanism is inclined to withdraw to-
wards the opposite extreme of otherworldly spirituality and
even to risk rendering itself inhuman by insisting on and
seeking refuge in the sanctioning primacy of the suprahu-
man, the unmaterialistic, the supernatural, the disembodied.
Certainly the Christian-humanist synthesis or integration of
Renaissance and Reformation found itself suspended on the
hyphenated horns of a dilemma. In the apparent disintegra-
tion of the seventeenth century, its tendency was to react
thence, against systematically sceptical materialism, in a

compensatory assertion of spirituality. *Paradise Lost*, as the compensatory vision of a blind and defeated poet and as a poem which descends into the dark and degenerate night of sinful perversity only to rise thence into the transcendent supernatural purity of timelessly holy light, can readily be interpreted as a major expression of this transcendentalizing process and as a text for illustrating the desirability of a similar response in our day.

I doubt the adequacy or the necessity of the interpretation, though there is of course much in Milton's career and in the superhuman machinery of his epic that can be made to lend support to it. There is, to begin with, the appearance of three-act tragic discontinuity in his career – the period of early poetic promise, when the Renaissance, the devotional, the baroque, are eloquently expressed but nowhere quite completely integrated, save perhaps in *Lycidas*; the twenty-year period of the controversial revolutionary prose, whose various principles, as they were elicited by discontinuous revolutionary crises, appear so difficult to organize into a coherent system, despite, perhaps because of, the conclusive controversiality of *De Doctrina Christiana*; and the post-Restoration years, which we habitually think of as years of blinded and defeated withdrawal, out of which the later poems spring, phoenix-like, as poems of compensatory, suprahuman assertion.

Indeed, the assumption of Miltonic discontinuity is nowadays so general and basic that, though the later poems are sometimes said to fulfil at large the promise of spirituality of the early poems, many commentaries on *Paradise Lost* can be conducted not only without reference to Milton's prose but without reference to his theological treatise which, in more historically pedantic days, used to be represented as an authoritative gloss on the epic. Milton writes, we are told, of things unattempted yet in prose or rhyme, of superhumanly heroic events in Heaven, of ideally unfallen human nature and its mythic Fall, even briefly in his last two books of the entire subsequent history of the human race, without any significant reference to the Civil War and the immense efforts of idealism and mind involved in it. We are asked to perceive that he does so because his later vision operates on a compensatingly higher level of pure spirituality, for which the demonic in Hell provides the contrast, of which Paradise is the mythic and disposable (because merely naturalistic) symbol, and to which Adam attains (through his fortunate fall and the rescuing office of the Son) in the visionary prophecies of the poem's last book. Even among some of the critics who are concerned to demonstrate the essentially biblical character of the later poems, we find an interpretation so spiritualized, in its opposition of spirit to letter, that it becomes not only supranatural and antinatural but suprarational and antirational. In terms of this evangel, the systematic theology of De Doctrina is the product of a Milton writing in intellectual chains and as of a devilishly intellectualizing party in proportion as his God the Father becomes a school divine. Thus we arrive at the implication, indeed the explicatory argument, that there is disjunction and discontinuity within Paradise Lost itself, between the mythologically or classically naturalistic and the supernaturally Christian, and further between the mechanical and unvitalized operations of intellect and transcendent poetic vision, or, as has lately been variously argued, between dogma and drama. And thus the reader is urged towards the vertically withdrawn serenity of a "paradise within thee, happier farr," instead of seeking to sustain the sense of a continuous and effective development of all the related human powers in relation to the divine purposes in as well as beyond time, which used to be represented as the typically Christian-humanist and Miltonic theme.

But it does not seem to me that Milton studies maintain their significant place as an important part of the work of our English departments simply because they offer, through the later poems, a compensatory escape from the burden and heat of our day to the dissociated. I think they rather maintain this place because the developing pattern of Milton's career, and the corpus of his writings, and not least *Paradise Lost*, transmit so much of what is creatively human and humanely inspiriting in the tradition of humanistic letters of which English departments these days are, for better or worse, the chief instruments.

This does not mean that I fail to appreciate the grandeurs, the splendours, or what the eighteenth century admired as the sublimity of the later poems and especially *Paradise Lost*. I would not discount the high soaring of Milton's by no means middle flight above the Aonian mount or the lofty height of his argument. I only argue that the spiritually epic proportions of his poetry, with its grand style and its loftiness of conception and setting, function, and were designed to function, to bring into highly illuminated relief an essentially human and humane significance that does not confirm withdrawal and dissociation but remains as relevant to the most humane endeavours of responsible human dignity, operating in and with time, as *Areopagitica* has been thought to be.

Nor does this mean that I fail of response to *Paradise Lost*'s representation of all the woe men experience despite, and along with, the advances of our civilization. I have to confess that, whenever I reread *Paradise Lost*, and always at some intermediate point in any semester's effort to induce a relevant response to it in students, I find myself incapable of avoiding dispiritedness and despair under the influence of its representation of enormous and destructive perversities and of sad human failure and misery. However little we may value, however much suspicion we may have of the irrelevance of the biographical approach, it is impossible not to reflect that what in the poem induces such despair is the shadow of the heavy weight of Milton's own frustrating experience. But evil days do not provide the main burden of the poem's narrative voice.

The poem consistently reflects, indeed illustrates, the archetypal patterns of the frustrating principalities and powers of darkness that appear to constitute the immediate context of human effort and experience. It concentrates our attention, in terms that remain immediately comprehensible to us despite the trans-shiftings of three centuries, on the patterns of human weakness and perversity which seem ever to make ultimate misery out of the most favourable opportunities and the most promising potentialities. It everywhere demands that we should face the inhuman and weakly human realities of the human situation. Indeed, it clearly designs, even through the parallelisms and contrasts established by its sublime grandeurs, to induce in us a despairing sense of such realities: (IX, 5–11)

> I now must change
> Those Notes to Tragic; foul distrust, and breach
> Disloyal on the part of Man, revolt,
> And disobedience: On the part of Heav'n
> Now alienated, distance and distaste,
> Anger and just rebuke, and judgement giv'n
> That brought into this World a world of woe ...

But this is not, I argue, the poem's final note; nor does it simply induce despair, or, to offset despair, a frantic leap outward into the mythomystically immense and suprahuman inane. On the contrary, and consistently with Milton's developing thinking in response to experience at every point, it reasserts, even so, the dignity and the potentiality of not only redeemed but restored and regenerated human nature in its proper and destined human sphere. It seems to me that the poem concludes thus for Adam and Eve, in the far from superfluous last books which lead directly into the patterns of ordinary experience. And it seems to me to maintain this bearing both in the large pattern of its structure and in the details which load every rift with refined ore.

As to its large pattern, I can only say (again) that the dis-position of its masses gives it, whether we are aware of this or not in the reading, the certainty of direction of a five-act dramatic structure. The arrangement of the given material, partly through the epic device of beginning in the apparent midst of affairs, partly through what has been chosen for significant elaboration, thus concentrates our attention on the human situation as that is typified by our first parents, unfallen, fallen, and recovered. The movement thus directed and controlled is everywhere inward to the human situation, not outward or upward away from what most concerns men, under the ways of God. The vertical reference, whether downward to Hell or upward to Heaven, is ultimately in the poem, and by a sort of poetic triangulation, chiefly signifi-cant in its bearing on the horizontal movement of the action in time.

The preliminary scenes in Hell and, more briefly, in Heaven, have their progressive attention fixed, through the progressive attention of their actors, on what is to become of Adam and Eve, and so of their progeny (among whom we are always included, as readers). The perverse Satanic re-covery of the two opening books, the first "act" – a parodic recovery through the misuse of God-permitted opportunity – characterizes the evil, the perverted use of God-given powers and opportunities, which is the apparently dominant factor in our woeful experience, existing as it did before man's creation. Heroic as are the dimensions of the represen-tation, it only serves to characterize, in massively impressive terms, the essential qualities of an evil we meet everywhere in our experience and find reflected in ourselves. Simile and metaphor, mythological, biblical, historical, and epic echoes and allusions serve at once to heighten our awareness of this and to realize yet more our familiarity with it. And we are, we know, involved in it, because we know that the horror that raises itself here is to impinge at once on human affairs in the attempt against God through man, and because we see

developing, with the parodic recovery, the preliminaries of
that attempt, and because – whether we accept the doctrine
of original sin or not – we know the desperate circumstances
surrounding human experience and endeavour, of which
these Hellish pseudo-grandeurs are the archetype. Yet, in the
perversely parodic recovery of Satan and his fellows, we
have – as nearly everyone nowadays would aver – the anti-
type of good. It is conventional now to observe that Satanic
heroism is the opposite of the heroism embodied in the Son,
and common nowadays to polarize the poem and its signifi-
cance in such simply opposed terms. Certainly, as foe to man
and as parodic prophet, popish priest, and tyrannous king,
Satan is a vicious parody of the Son as mediator between his
Father and fallen men. But Satan's perverted recovery, under
God's high permission, is also gigantically parodic of the
recovery that is open to fallen men through the actions of
the Mediator. His revival on the burning lake, his uprising,
and his recollection of his powers and his purposes, dread-
fully caricature the process through which we may be re-
stored by "one greater man." His ascent into created light is
a cosmic parody of the experience of illumination through
the light that lighteth every man that cometh into the world.

That light, in its various levels of effective manifestation
and rather than a simply supranatural light, seems to me the
theme of the great invocation opening the poem's third book
and therewith the second "act" (BOOKS III and IV), which
presents us with scenes of observation, first in Heaven, then
of the harmoniously created universe (as Satan explores it
and, disguisedly, contemplates it with the help of Uriel, the
angel of the Sun), and finally of Adam and Eve in Paradise.
Whatever may be the problems presented to our modern
readings by Milton's God – and, especially in his theological
assertiveness, and to judge from the harsh comments that
are almost uniformly made on him and on Milton's lapses in
poetic tact in this connection, this is for us a chief crux of the
poem – whatever may be the problems presented to us by

the debatable scene in Heaven, its observations are focussed, by the very fact that the Almighty Father bends "down his eye, / His own works and their works at once to view" (III, 358–9), on the developing Satanic endeavour and on the destiny, evil and fortunate, that awaits man. The Son's resolution of the crux of justice and mercy is of course the prime concern of the scene in Heaven; but this resolution bears squarely on and is firmly referred to the human situation; and, in being prophetic of the Incarnation (whose characterization, in Gospels and Epistles, it anticipates, or rather echoes), it makes of the Son not only a mediator but an imitable type whose example is of significance as to both unfallen and recovered men. Of the powers and purposes in the nature of things that make for uprightness and recovery, the Satanic exploration of creation gives us a sufficient impression, as context for the paradisal human situation, a contextual impression which will subsequently be enlarged by Raphael's account of the creation. This throws into the sharpest contrasting relief, both as to the divine creative intention, and as to the human situation with respect to that, the Satanic refusal, at the beginning of BOOK IV, of the opportunity of redemption through a realigning of effort with what the Satanic recovery and exploration have themselves demonstrated to be the essentially creative nature of things. The contrast – subsequently elaborated in Raphael's reminiscential account of the War in Heaven – renders Satan the type of those, among angels or men, who refuse to fulfil themselves by aligning their efforts with the divine creative purposes. It also defines the type of such dynamic alignment which we have seen in the Son and find in its initially human form in the activities and the contemplations of our unfallen first parents in BOOK IV.

The poem's opening acts have thus provided the more-than-cosmic framework of its human concerns, while steadily focussing in upon these. From BOOK IV onward, apart from brief scenes in Heaven and Hell which incidentally reassert this context, our attention is concentrated on the human situation, unfallen, fallen, and recovered. The point of reference is however always, even in the representation of unfallen man, what it has been from the beginning and through the scenes in Hell and Heaven – the human situation as it is now in the time of our reading, after man's first disobedience and in the midst of woe, yet under the hope that we may have "till one greater Man / Restore us." (I, 4–5) Simile and mythological and literary allusion continue to remind us of that point of reference for the poem's significance. It is perhaps this allusion which makes us complain incidentally of the poem's rigidly structured parts, of its discordant tones, and especially of its insistent doctrinal preoccupations, when we attempt to read it simply as an effort to reproduce and recapture in some visionary way the atmosphere and attitude of the innocently paradisal state; or alternatively induces some commentators to believe that the paradisal books already demonstrate, in greater or less degree, the woeful human weaknesses and perversities that make the Fall not only certain but inevitable, showing it to be so not only already with the account of Eve's Narcissistic response to her creation, as it is described by her in BOOK IV, but even in the contemplative questionings about the divine creative purpose that are raised there, and even more so in the human response to paradisal experience and to Raphael's relation of what has transpired before the coming of man to consciousness, the War in Heaven and the process of Creation, in the four central, paradisal books, V to VIII, which seem to me to constitute the third and central "act" of the dramatic structure.

Despite the expanse of imagination Raphael's accounts demand of Adam and us, the essential point of reference remains the developing human situation. We should perhaps reflect, more than we habitually do, that when Raphael says he will try to solve his problem of communication by likening things in Heaven to things on Earth, since they may indeed

be liker than may at first be thought (v, 570–6), he is point-
ing to his effort to illuminate the human situation by setting
it in the context of perversely Satanic and divinely creative
endeavour. It is with man's creative place in the scheme of
things that Raphael is concerned in his discussions of the
scale of nature or the relation between human and angelic
being. Indeed, from the beginning of this section of the
poem – with Adam's comment on Eve's contact with evil
through the dream induced by Satan – we are concerned with
a developing human experience that involves the recognition
of the character of evil as the perverting of potential good,
and thus moreover with the complex psychology of the
human response to experience.

Perhaps the most significant and rewarding development
in Milton commentary of late lies in our debates over and
reconsiderations of these central, paradisal books of the
poem. We are recognizing the significance of the fact that,
unlike so many of his more simple-minded, nostalgic, or
pessimistically idealizing contemporaries (and unlike so
many of his modern critics), Milton did not think of or
represent even the paradisal state as static in total perfection.
His Adam and Eve are, as he often says, innocent and, in
their way and in the terms appropriate to their stage and
situation, perfect. But "perfect" in this sense does not, we
see, mean absolutely complete and fulfilled. They are gifted
sufficiently for their situation, as God's harshest lines of
condemnation assert; yet, harsh as they are, the lines also
imply a free responsibility for creative self-development:
(III, 97–106)

> ingrate, he had of mee
> All he could have; I made him just and right,
> Sufficient to have stood, though free to fall ...
> Not free, what proof could they have givn sincere
> ...
> Of true allegiance, constant Faith or Love,
> Where onely what they needs must do, appeard,
> Not what they would ...

Many commentators on the poem evidently think that God should have provided our first parents not only with all they "could have" in their circumstances and according to the divine creative purposes, which made man an image of God not least in creative potentiality, but with an impregnable and absolute perfection such as even Milton's angels do not possess. But we understand that this would have been contrary to, indeed would have been to stultify, the divine creative purpose, not only as to the freedom of will of creatures but as to their dynamic fulfilment of those freely creative powers in which the reflected image of God chiefly lies. Thus what is significant about unfallen Adam and Eve is that they are in an innocent state of nature whose potentialities are to be developed, with forethought and joy, such as is indicated by the cultivation of the fertile garden, to which Adam was removed out of mere nature, and by the expectation of an increasing progeny.

Indeed, though some commentators are to be found still regarding the responses of our first parents, to their paradisal situation and the confrontations that occur in it, as chiefly symptomatic of fatal human weakness, we have come to see, even in Eve's counterpoised Narcissism, or in her recoiling recovery from her Satan-induced dream, or in Adam's demand for a mate in permitted argument with God, or in his tendency to exaggerated eloquence in the expression of his love for her, occasions on which both the knowledge of self and the recognition of the divine purposes, both the sense of potentiality and the sense of related responsibility, are furthered and developed towards an increasing perfection.

Raphael, on the scale of nature, is nowadays often quoted in testimony to this dramatically developmental significance of the paradisal state: (v, 496–503)

> from these corporal nutriments perhaps
> Your bodies may at last turn all to Spirit,
> Improv'd by tract of time, and wingd ascend

> Ethereal, as wee, or may at choice
> Here or in Heav'nly Paradises dwell;
> If ye be found obedient, and retain
> Unalterably firm his love entire
> Whose progenie you are ...

Adam himself, by an immediate question, underlines the importance of the cautionary condition as to a dynamic, filially loving obedience. But Michael's testimony, after the Fall has occurred and has inhibited the paradisal potentialities, seems to me even more striking and relevant. It is possible to misread Raphael, as expressing the notion of a sort of spontaneously Neoplatonic ascent out of the natural, repudiating and denying (rather than improving) it, into a transcendent realm of pure spirituality – though the weight of the poem hitherto should have taught us that to be truly angelic is not radically different from being truly and completely human, and though both the alternative of "Here" and the unchanging condition should underline the principle of continuity. Michael's companion notation for the benefit of fallen Adam, of what the cultivation of now lost Paradise might have resulted in, seems to me to provide a sounder perspective, for it at once contrasts the postlapsarian with the prelapsarian situation and insists on the continuity, for the recovered, of sustaining power and, under that, potentialities: (XI, 335–54)

> *Adam*, thou know'st Heav'n his, and all the Earth,
> Not this Rock onely; his Omnipresence fills
> Land, Sea, and Aire, and every kinde that lives,
> Fomented by his virtual power and warmd:
> All th' Earth he gave thee to possess and rule,
> No despicable gift; surmise not then
> His presence to these narrow bounds confin'd
> Of Paradise or *Eden*: this had been
> Perhaps thy Capital Seate, from whence had spred
> All generations, and had hither come

From all the ends of th' Earth, to celebrate
And reverence thee thir great Progenitor.
But this præeminence thou hast lost, brought down
To dwell on eeven ground now with thy Sons:
Yet doubt not but in Vallie and in plaine
God is as here, and will be found alike
Present, and of his presence many a signe
Still following thee, still compassing thee round
With goodness and paternal Love, his Face
Express, and of his steps the track Divine.

This infrequently quoted passage from the eleventh book formulates, Michael says, the faith in which Adam is to be confirmed before he is expelled from Paradise. Like many other passages in the last books of the poem, it emphasizes the continuity of supported endeavour, despite woeful change, that Adam and all his sons are called to. If the passage sets fallen Adam firmly on a level with his sons, it also implies that restored man may yet find himself upheld "On even ground against his mortal foe." (III, 179) And its contrasts serve to underline the creative endeavours to which unfallen Adam was already called, for his and Eve's self-fulfilment and the fulfilment of his progeny.

In the central, paradisal books, we see Adam and Eve innocently proceeding in this direction, through the developing powers of mind and body, in incident after prelapsarian incident. It may in due course even prove possible to argue that Eve's desire to work alone (near the beginning of BOOK IX) – which gives Satan the wished-for occasion for his attempt, and which currently presents us with one of the most serious cruxes confronting our interpretative endeavours – is a perfectly legitimate, if hazardous (but all such situations are hazardous in the unfallen or the fallen state) expression of justifiably growing and developing human (if feminine) individuality.

But of course with this incident we are on the verge of the

Fall, in BOOK IX, with its consequences in BOOK X, the climactic fourth "act" of the drama. If our rereading of the central and paradisal books begins to concentrate our attention on the note of developing potentiality, that only serves, at first sight, to increase the terrible and tragic impact of the Fall's disastrous perversion of potentiality, and the impact of all our woe under an experience in which we ever find potentiality somehow not only lamentably unfulfilled but even most dreadfully perverted, and most efficacious not in its dynamic but in its demonic consequences.

And yet the Satanically induced Fall is perhaps, like the Satanic itself, chiefly and finally significant for what it parodies. We are conscious not only of all that was lost by it, of all the frustrations and perversities that spring from or are typified by it, but of the Fall as involving a lost opportunity for self-development and further self-fulfilment. For the Milton of *De Doctrina* the temptation of the good is always primarily a testing opportunity, and an insistently demanding calling. (*Works* xv, 87–9) Perhaps the Fall may be seen as the consequence of such a temptation even more readily in its dramatically epic representation than in the eleventh chapter of the first book of the treatise. Those romantic critics among us who can only find it in their hearts to praise Eve for aspiration, and especially to praise Adam for romantically loving self-sacrifice, induce us to consider the alternatives open to both, and especially to Adam. And thereby they teach us, unintentionally, to consider the process of the Fall as essentially a perverting parody of a potential process already adumbrated in the poem, by the resolutions of the Son in BOOK III and, in a degree, by unfallen Adam and Eve themselves.

Though it is perhaps a feat that requires more talent, certainly more time, than I have, it is not necessary to underemphasize Milton's despairing and painful concern with the Fall and all the woe derivative from it, his pained sensibility in the representation of the processes of perversity and its consequences, in order to maintain that this representation yet operates, by parodic contrast and by its relation to the parodic evil of the poem's two opening books, to enforce the creative and recreative norm that has been represented by the Son and potentially illustrated by the paradisal books. What is more, the fourth act of the drama is not simply concerned with the Fall and its woeful consequences. It is punctuated by the prophetic judgment of Adam and Eve and the serpent by the Son; and the second half of the act, BOOK X, represents not simply the despair of Adam and Eve but the partial working out of the significance of the just yet promisingly prophetic and merciful judgment through which prevenient grace begins its work of softening stony hearts and teaching obedience. Eve, as we all now recognize (after Mr. Tillyard and other commentators), makes her contribution to this by wishing sacrificially to take the blame and punishment upon herself. But I am glad we have the testimony of women such as Mrs. Mary Ann Nevins Radzinowicz,[1] to support us in recognizing that it is Adam, perceiving that the acceptance of blame and punishment is not all they are called to, who works the matter out towards the repentance which marks a crucial turning point in the process of restoration. The intensely dramatic soliloquy – whose meditations on despair and guilt and death and prophesied grace Mr. Svendsen has so effectively analyzed[2] – is clearly no less than the process of the Fall or the earlier Satanic soliloquizing resolution in favour of despair and evil, one of the high dramatic moments of the poem, underlined as such by being prelude to the repentant prayers with which BOOK X and the fourth act conclude. The repentance itself is prelude to the restorative, though painful as well as wonderful, process that is the matter of the final book of the

1 Mary N. Radzinowicz, "Eve and Dalila: Renovation and Hardening of the Heart," *Reason and the Imagination*, ed. J. A. Mazzeo (New York 1962), 171–2.
2 Kester Svendsen, "Adam's Soliloquy in BOOK X of *Paradise Lost*," *College English*, x (1949), 366–70.

poem in 1667 or of its last two books and so of its final, fifth "act" in 1674, that part of the poem which prepares Adam and Eve for their expulsion from Paradise into the world we know and in terms of which the whole has been developed.

Though the effort goes back at least to a now very old essay by the late E. N. S. Thompson[3] and has some intervening support in speculations about the structural pattern of the poem, one of the most remarkable preoccupations of recent commentary is represented by the critical effort of late to make more effective and relevant sense of the significance of these last books, with their vision of sin and prophecy of redemptive incarnation, sacrifice, and ultimately conclusive triumph, than earlier commentary was able to make.[4] We are led to recognize how necessary and organic to the whole, despite their brevity, these books are. What seems most striking about these efforts is that they demonstrate not simply how vision and prophecy fill out and complete the cycle and pattern of history but how these induce the further extension of Adam's response to experience and prepare him to face, with equanimity if also with profound sadness, the experience of the fallen world on which he must enter. And, by way of dream, Eve's response also.

If in these books our attention is concentrated, like Adam's through Michael's agency, on the variously horrifying and depressing scenes of wickedness and perversity and then on the elements of the prophetic summary of the process of redemption, yet what guides or ought to guide our response is the developing character of Adam's response. Here, as in the paradisal books and by parody in the accounts of the falls, the essential centre of attention lies in the exemplary response of the drama's principal person to the experience represented. And here we may find, after further

3 E. N. S. Thompson, "For *Paradise Lost*, XI–XII," *PQ*, XXII (1943), 376–82.
4 *Milton: Modern Essays in Criticism*, ed. Arthur E. Barker (New York 1965), editor's note, 356.

scholarly analysis and critical reflection, yet further and most significant evidence of the organic relation between the poem's message and its medium, between Miltonic dogma and drama. What Adam's responses illustrate is the developing process of restorative response to the central fact of the divine creative purpose and the divine love and mercy which has everywhere been the poem's chief concern, whether parodically in terms of perversity, or by direct analogy in terms of the prelapsarian state, or now in the representation of preparative recovery.

This is only brought into sharper relief by the epic divisions of the twelve-book poem of 1674, in which the theme of fallen degeneracy is regularly counterpoised by and subordinated to the theme of continually sustaining creative and recreative power. The parodic Satanic recovery of the first two books is balanced and defined in its degeneracy by the scenes in Heaven, the Creation, and Paradise in the third and fourth books. Raphael's account of the War in Heaven in v and vi is balanced by his account of the Creation and the discussion of it in vii and viii. The representation of the Fall and of both its woeful and its cathartic consequences is balanced by the recovery, parodically implied in the Fall itself, which is begun under the prevenient grace of judgment in x and represented in preparation for our world in xi and xii.

It seems to be possible, and indeed necessary, to recognize that the details everywhere contribute continuously and consistently to the realizing of this effect, while at the same time insisting on the reality of that woe which Milton thought chiefly functioned not simply as punishment but as an instrument of the catharsis which should reorient us to the creative process in the nature of things. This seems to me, for instance, and despite all the complaints we hear nowadays of Milton's God, even from the most admiringly spiritualized readers, the point of that scene in Heaven in BOOK III where the Father formulates progressively the theological principles which the poem's action embodies and realizes. I must express my more than editorial agreement with what Mrs. Stella Purce Revard demonstrates to be the organic relations between dogma and drama in this scene.[5] I am persuaded by Mrs. Revard's argument that the scene is designed to throw into the fullest dramatic relief the exemplary and freely loving response of the Son, to the Father's merciful purposes, the response of an independent and responsible person, in terms of that freedom of will which the Son possesses according to the subordinationist view of his relation to the Father which Mr. William B. Hunter, Jr., has shown Milton to have derived from earlier Greek theology.[6] To what Mrs. Revard has said of the crucial and exemplary process of mind by which the Son is represented as freely and actively bringing his will into recreative line with what he knows, despite the appearances of mere justice, to be the loving and merciful purpose of the Father as to his creatures, there is nothing to add. Our difficulties with Milton's God would be greatly lessened if we recognized and adequately appraised the dramatic role which the Father purposely adopts in order to challenge the Son and to induce from him a loving and sacrificial response, as his ways challenge all beings to make creative use of proffered opportunity. And I would add that the adoption of this role to induce such a response is designed to set the stage for the Father's formulation of the recreative and restorative theological principles central to the poem.

At the beginning of this scene, God and the Son bend down their eyes to contemplate God's works and their works, and, beyond the joy and love of unfallen Adam and Eve, the rage that transports the Adversary as he makes his

5 Stella P. Revard, "The Dramatic Function of the Son in *Paradise Lost*: A Commentary on Milton's 'Trinitarianism'," *JEGP*, LXVI (1967), 45–58.
6 William B. Hunter, Jr., "Milton's Arianism Reconsidered," *HTR*, LII (1959), 9–35.

way from the edge of chaos down through the spheres of the created universe. I suggest that – with an irony we find difficult of acceptance through our tenderly idealizing inclinations, yet an irony which is an essential element in the poem's comment on perverse and degenerate effort, Satanic or human – God chooses to adopt the tone and role of the merely wrathful deity that Satan, in his perverse impercipience, supposes him to be and has been represented as supposing him to be in the poem's opening books. The Father does so in order to induce from the Son what he knows will be thus induced by contrast – a dynamically percipient response founded on a clear sense of what the divine character really is and what the divine creative purposes for all willing creatures really are. In this representation of the Father's ironic adoption of a Satanically conceived role, the scene challenges us. It challenges us to recognize that the Son is exemplary in becoming the true image of his Father and the embodiment of the poem's main theme, through his recognition, his foresight, and his willing acceptance of his recreative role under the Father's purposes, in sharpest contrast to the dreadful idol of self-assertion Satan would raise. Our common inclination is to think that Milton's God is simply self-assertive and self-justifying in this scene. But it seems possible to see him as here willing to take upon himself the form of a merely wrathful deity in order to provide the Son with an opportunity to show what the Father is confident he will show, that justice is essentially an instrument of mercy.

And the scene should also thus, by its progressive development, concentrate our attention not only on man's free-willed responsibility for his own Fall, but on what the Son's response elicits from the Father, the statement of purposes not only redemptive but restorative and regenerative for such as imitate the Son's example in response to the divine love and mercy: (III, 173–97)

Man shall not quite be lost, but sav'd who will,
Yet not of will in him, but grace in me
Freely voutsaft; once more I will renew
His lapsed powers, though forfeit and enthrall'd
By sin to foul exorbitant desires;
Upheld by me, yet once more he shall stand
On even ground against his mortal foe,
By me upheld, that he may know how frail
His fall'n condition is, and to me ow
All his deliv'rance, and to none but me.
Some I have chosen of peculiar grace
Elect above the rest; so is my will:
The rest shall hear me call, and oft be warnd
Thir sinful state, and to appease betimes
Th' incensed Deitie, while offerd grace
Invites; for I will cleer thir senses dark,
What may suffice, and soft'n stonie hearts
To pray, repent, and bring obedience due.
To Prayer, repentance, and obedience due,
Though but endevord with sincere intent,
Mine ear shall not be slow, mine eye not shut.
And I will place within them as a guide
My Umpire *Conscience*, whom if they will hear,
Light after light well us'd they shall attain,
And to the end persisting, safe arrive.

Parodically in terms of fall and degeneracy, by analogy (with
difference) in terms of the developing prelapsarian state, by
representation in its last books, this, I suggest, is the con-
tinuously relevant and demanding theme of the poem. It is,
I suggest, what we hear echoing in the poem's difficult but
heartening close, as it has echoed continuously, and with no
discontinuity or disjunction throughout. It perhaps echoes
chiefly in Michael's performance of his office and in Adam's
response to this. It echoes not least, at any rate, in Adam's

declaration that he has learned that to obey is best and to love with fear the only God, observing his providence and depending on his mercy, as the Redeemer's example teaches (XII, 561–73). It echoes no less in Michael's conclusive exhortation to "add deeds" to this knowledge "answerable" in expectation of attaining that "paradise within" which is perhaps chiefly and after all the good conscience resulting from endeavouring in faith with sincere intent (XII, 581–7). And it seems to me to be also the central and continuous theme both of Milton's prose and of his theological treatise.

As to the prose, I can only aver that the massive historical and thematic analysis and annotation of its blocks with which we are in process of being provided has the effect of bringing into relief for me the central point at which Milton differed from most of his contemporaries and successors, in arguing that dynamic reforms on the natural or domestic or political levels must depend on the spiritual and thence ethical regeneration of Englishmen. And in this connection I would say that, whereas Whig or liberal and more recently radical interpretations of the prose tell us that its central preoccupation is with liberty, our own politicians and agitators might find it more to their purpose than they do if they recognized that its preoccupation is rather with responsive and responsible effort, with the qualifications – consistent with those demanded of men by Milton's God or by Michael of Adam – necessary for the exercise of a responsible freedom or a free responsibility. If the effort to translate this into revolutionary institutional terms met with frustration, it is nevertheless reasserted by God and by Michael in thoroughly human, if uninstitutionalized, terms. Our tendency to identify human history with merely institutional history perhaps obscures for us the fact that, despite its gloom, Michael's representation of human history makes it a God-directed process designed to elicit a response of free responsibility on all the levels of activity represented by the relations between Adam and Eve and what is implied of their relations with their immediate progeny – and so of our relations.

The regenerated response, under grace, of a free responsibility is, I submit, certainly the main preoccupation of *De Doctrina*, regarded as the conclusion of the prose effort or as a systematic preparation for the later poems. We might see this simply from the shape of its first book, and we might judge from thence the essential bearing of all those striking heresies in Milton's theology which naturally attract our abstractly scholarly attention but do so in a way which tends to divert our attention from the main matter in hand throughout *De Doctrina*. Those fascinating heresies – whether about the doctrine of accommodation, or about the divine decrees, or about the relation between the divine persons, or about creation *de Deo* rather than *ex nihilo* – all chiefly present themselves in the first seven of the first fourteen chapters of the treatise that are now extant, in the manuscript in the Record Office, in a fair copy made after Milton's death by Daniel Skinner. It has been said that Skinner must have had to recopy these chapters (with a view to their publication which was frustrated by Restoration authority) because they were so heavily revised; and it has been assumed that these chapters must contain the principles peculiarly characteristic of Milton's thought.

But the first thirteen chapters of the treatise are preliminary to its main matter. If they were heavily revised, they were probably so revised to bring them into coherent line with the chapters concerning this main matter, which include references back to the principal heresies and themselves have been revised with some care, as we can see in the manuscript. And that main matter is, in fact, firmly asserted in the fourth chapter of the book, when Milton, in connection with the conditional character of all the divine decrees, roundly and at length refutes the Calvinistic doctrine of the predestination of the elect and formulates those principles of conditionality and of responsibility that are summarized so accurately in the speech of God in BOOK III of *Paradise Lost*, from which I have quoted at length. Chapter 14 of the treatise comes to "Man's Restoration, wherein of Redemption; and of Christ as Redeemer." The remaining nineteen chapters of the treatise's first book concern themselves with the various aspects of the process of redemption and of renovation and regeneration, which are the treatise's main concerns. Restoration and renovation, through redemption, and regeneration, through the response of faith to redemptive grace, provide the renewed and extended powers through which fallen men can manage to perform those duties to God and their neighbours which are the subjects of the treatise's still insufficiently emphasized second book (and of Michael's closing exhortations to Adam).

I suggest that the striking heresies of the treatise's opening chapters, with whatever extensive revision we may assume there, exist because of their bearing on Milton's conception of the process of renovation and regeneration through grace. The heresy as to the freely willing subordinationist Son exists because Christ must be not only redeemer but an exemplar of the creatively responsive cooperation God desires of his creatures; and the heresies about the Creation exist to underline what is asserted of man in that connection – that he is a being intrinsically one, and not divisible into body and soul or between natural and spiritual – because salvation involved for Milton, as his God says in the epic's third book, the renovation in sufficient degree of the natural powers of understanding and willing, and the regenerate extension, on that basis, of supranatural (but not therefore antinatural) powers. This process of renovation and regeneration simply constitutes Milton's view of religious experience. Though his sense of this process has some analogy to the developing theories of revolutionary Protestant radicals like the extreme Independent John Goodwin or the semi-millenarian Henry Vane, and to the practical piety of some Anglicans and of Richard Baxter, and also to the rationalism of the Cambridge divines, I do not find that anyone in the period – dominated as it was by the varieties of the Calvinistic segregation of grace and salvation from the natural – presents with anything like Milton's systematic insistence, precision, and elaboration, such a conception of the progressive experience of restoration and regeneration as depending, through grace, repentance, and efforts of will and understanding, on the progressive restoration of natural human powers for their progressive extension and perfecting in the regeneratedly spiritual.

I suggest, too, that this unifying conception informs the whole of *Paradise Lost* and is the central point of reference for its parodies, analogies, and exemplars. What is essential to the conception is, first, Milton's insistence that, through prevenient grace and its initial calling, redemption operates for all men, not simply for a predestined spiritual elect. All men – including pagans who have not heard of Christ, as we may judge from the virtuous among them and from Adam's partial recovery in BOOK X – are, by God's mercy and through Christ's mediation, set on sufficiently even ground with their adversary by the gracious restoration to them, in sufficient degree, of the power of natural understanding and the natural freedom of will which were sacrificed at the Fall. All men are thus called by God's mercy to some sense of responsibility, to some knowledge of the way in which God would be worshipped and propitiated, to some sense of their deficiencies, and to some sense of the need for redemptive support and for a positively repentant and imitative response to it. If, at the end of the revolution, *De Doctrina* is pessimistic about the number of those who heed this call and in whom repentance and faith and renovation are more than merely temporary, yet it is a call made by grace to and through natural human powers and involving an appraisal of actual human experience and effort. In those who through their natural powers give heed to it, progress in true repen-

tance and sustained and sustaining faith depends on this
partial and progressive restoration and renovation of natural
powers, not on their repudiation in favour of supernatural
powers. The supernatural regeneration which follows when
the initial call is heeded adds to the renovated natural
powers, comparable to prelapsarian Adam's, the spiritual
powers Adam might have attained to without woe, had he
not fallen.

De Doctrina's definition, at the beginning of its chapter on
regeneration, is firm and exact: (*Works*, xv, 367)

> The intent of Supernatural Renovation is not only to re-
> store man more completely than before to the use of his
> natural faculties, as regards his power to form right
> judgment, and to exercise free will; but to create afresh,
> as it were, the inward man, and infuse from above new and
> supernatural faculties into the minds of the renovated.
> This is called Regeneration, and the regenerate are said to
> be planted in Christ.
>
> Regeneration is that change operated by the Word and
> the Spirit, whereby the old man being destroyed, the in-
> ward man is regenerated by God after his own image, in
> all the faculties of his mind, insomuch that he becomes as
> it were a new creature, and the whole man is sanctified
> both in body and soul, for the service of God, and the
> performance of good works.

It seems to me that everything else in Milton's treatise leads
towards or depends on the Miltonic conception of religious
experience here defined. For the process leads, as *De Doc-
trina* makes clear, to the enjoyment of a progressively de-
veloping Christian liberty having (whatever the perversity
of the world's institutions) natural as well as spiritual privi-
leges and responsibilities. It does so because it involves the
effective rewriting in the hearts of believers of that vital and
unwritten law which is the law of God's creative intention
for his creatures. "The unwritten law is no other than that

law of nature given originally to Adam, and of which a certain remnant, or imperfect illumination, still dwells in the hearts of all mankind; which, in the regenerate, under the influence of the Holy Spirit, is daily tending towards a renewal of its primitive brightness" (*Works*, XVI, 101). *In regeneratis vero spiritus sancti opera indies ad perfectionem primaevam renovatur*: the note of progressive renovation, in the time which is God's instrument and man's opportunity, not his punishment, will be found to be fully sustained everywhere in the treatise's Latin, even more than in Sumner's translation.

It seems to me that such passages as these do indeed gloss the divine pronouncements of *Paradise Lost*, if these need any gloss apart from the poem's representations. What *Paradise Lost* represents in the end is a process of progressively humanizing education, issuing in appropriately humane actions. For, says *De Doctrina*, "Undoubtedly, if to believe be to act, faith is an action, or rather a frame of mind acquired and confirmed by a succession of actions, although in the first instance infused from above. ..." (*Works*, XVI, 35) Hence Michael's exhortation to Adam to add to an obedience which is not, as Satan thinks, merely a matter of "submission," deeds to his knowledge answerable. And here, with reference to such action and considering the organic relation between medium and message, I would note how very dramatic, rather than how transcendentally mythomystic, the essential Miltonic conception is, both as to the educative development, through experience, of the individual and in the implied relations between the individual and others.

The representations of *Paradise Lost* more than adequately convey the drama of such actions. We have been taught to see this most clearly in the representation of the parodic actions of Satan. But I would think we have yet to appraise adequately the extent to which the heroic or epic is everywhere dramatized to make it the significant framework for the drama of human experience represented at the poem's centre, and the extent to which that representation of experience everywhere echoes and makes use of the modes of Elizabethan and Jacobean drama, domestic, revenge, romantic, tragic, or problematical. If in *De Doctrina*, because of a mode of discourse to which we are antipathetic, the Miltonic principles tend – to use a phrase of Sidney's – to "lie dark before the imaginative and judging power," the mimetic character of their depiction in *Paradise Lost* makes them immediately relevant to our human experience, by a process of representing, counterfeiting, or figuring forth which is in a sense a culmination not only of the narrative and lyric but more especially of the dramatic Renaissance literary tradition.

Milton did not sacrifice this, any more than any other essentially creative element in the traditions he inherited, when he wrote *Paradise Lost*. And his essential dogmas are so far from inhibiting drama that his conception of progressive regeneration, natural and spiritual, through the rhythmic and repeated operation of repentance and faith, contrition and conversion to good, and his conception of the human works of faith in which regeneration issues, demand dramatic constitutions for their adequate expression.

The essential effect of *Paradise Lost* depends on the mimetic representation of the conflict of motives and values and purposes in the minds of its characters, and especially on their active relations everywhere to one another. Considering the web of dramatically represented relations, in organically related and dynamically developing scene after scene, it is difficult to see how the figures of *Paradise Lost* (or of the other two later poems) can be regarded as exemplars of painful or exalted isolation. Some of course would isolate themselves if they could. But it is Satan who mistakenly asserts that "The mind is its own place" and can in itself "make a Heav'n of Hell" (I, 254–5). Even Satan is, perversely, what he is because of his broken relations with God and the Son and the angels, and his relations with his fellows and Adam and Eve. The Son is what he is because of his relations with his Father and with all creatures, who have been created and are sustained through him, and especially with men, fallen and recovered. And the core of the poem concerns and everywhere depends on the developing relations between Adam and Eve and the Son and God, and not least what must reflect the relations of Adam and Eve with the Son and God, their relations with each other and with that progeny (which imaginatively includes ourselves) whose fortunes run as a constant thread through the poem.

"MOST PERFECT HERO"

The Role of the Son in Milton's Theodicy

HUGH MACCALLUM

Milton lived in an age of theodicies. Arminians and Socinians, Oxford rationalists and Cambridge Platonists, all sought to humanize the abstract theology of Protestant orthodoxy. Reacting against the stern Calvinist doctrines of faith and predestination, they attempted to justify the ways of God to man by showing that those ways are reasonable and consistent with the highest moral ideals known by the light of nature. Benjamin Whichcote, Milton's contemporary at Cambridge, spoke for the whole liberalizing movement in his observation that "when God demands and challenges 'Are not my wayes equal?' " he appeals "to man's principles and rules, whereby he is able to discerne and judge; whereby God shall be justified, and Man convinced."[1] It is precisely

1 *Moral and religious aphorisms ... to which are added eight letters which passed between Dr. Whichcote and Dr. Tuckney*, ed. Samuel Salter (London 1753), 45.

this principle which informs Milton's two studies in theo-
dicy, his theological treatise, *De Doctrina Christiana*, and his
epic, *Paradise Lost*.

Central to most theodicies of the period was the role of
the Son of God. The conflict between the new rationalism
and the old orthodoxy found its matrix in those doctrines
which concern the nature and office of Christ. Anthony
Tuckney, who attempted to uphold the primacy of faith
against the liberalizing movement inspired by his former
pupil, Whichcote, complains of those "sublimated *Deists* of
our Age, who, it seemeth, are such intimate friends of God,
that they can have free access to him, without a Mediator."[2]
At the other end of the scale of Protestant attitudes we
might place George Fox, who also sought, according to his
own lights, to emphasize the Son's significance. The West-
minster Assembly of divines, Fox notes, has "laid down ...
That the holy Ghost and the Son is equall in power and glory
with the Father"; and yet, he goes on, "if anyone come to
witnesse the Son revealed in him ... or ... the minde of Christ,
and witness that equal with the Father ... you Priests cry out
horrid Blasphemy."[3] Tuckney, with his Calvinist conception
of the operation of grace, finds the meaning of Christ in the
sacrifice by which he makes expiation for man's sin and thus
reconciles God to men. Fox, with his evangelical emphasis on
the inner light, finds the meaning of Christ in his restoration
of the image of God in man by the illumination of man's
mind and the regeneration of his will. Is Christ then an advo-
cate and ransom for us, or is he a principle of grace in us? Is
his office priestly or prophetic? And is he to be seen as a
model of patience and heroic martyrdom, or as the super-
natural being who satisfies the justice of God by a sacrifice
which cannot be imitated by mankind? It was over such
issues that the new, liberalizing theology, whether humanis-

2 *None but Christ, or a Sermon upon Acts 4.12 ...* (London 1654), 45.
3 *The Great Mistery of the Great Whore Unfolded ...* (London
   1659), 67.

tic or evangelical, came into conflict with the ideas of Reformation orthodoxy.

In a period of such controversy, Milton set out to write an epic poem that would justify the ways of God to men and that took the Son of God as one of its major characters. It is thus not surprising that the roles of the Son in *Paradise Lost* are extraordinarily varied and rich in significance. In Raphael's narrative of the antecedent action, we are shown the pre-existent Son, the Logos; in Michael's narrative of subsequent action, we are shown the Incarnate Son, the God-man; while the poet himself presents, in dramatic form, the events in Heaven that lead the pre-existent Son to undertake the task of redeeming mankind by assuming human nature. The poem thus covers all the major areas of theological controversy about the Son, including the Trinity, the Incarnation, and the nature of the Atonement.

Considering the various manifestations of the Son chronologically, in the sequence in which they occur rather than the sequence in which they are presented in the poem, the first takes place on a feast day in Heaven. The Father, addressing the Empyreal host from his flaming mount, introduces new laws and a new dispensation for the angels: (v, 602–6)

> Hear my Decree, which unrevok't shall stand.
> This day I have begot whom I declare
> My onely Son, and on this holy Hill
> Him have anointed, whom ye now behold
> At my right hand; your Head I him appoint ...

He does not mean, of course, that he has just created the Son; indeed, as Abdiel points out, the Son existed before the angels and was their creator. The Father has begotten the Son in the metaphoric sense of having raised him to this new position of Lordship over the angels.[4] The Son himself

---

4 See *De Doctrina Christiana, Works*, xiv, 181. For an interpretation of Milton's views on this subject, see Maurice Kelley, *This Great Argument* (Princeton 1941), 94 ff.

remains curiously passive during this ceremony, denying any words of reassurance to his new subjects, and this silence, coupled with the emphasis on the implacable will of the Father, draws attention to the manner in which the obedience of the angels is now being tested. The faithful Abdiel sees in the Son's acceptance of his new role an act of divine humility by which all the angels are made more illustrious: "since he the Head / One of our number thus reduc't becomes, / His Laws our Laws, all honour to him done / Returns our own ... " (v, 842–5) Thus the Son's act is made to foreshadow his later assumption of the form of a servant to save mankind. Satan, on the other hand, sees in the change of government an unforgivable instance of the Father's nepotism. By an act of tyrannical power, he believes, his equal has been exalted to a position of authority over him. His refusal to accept the "yoke / Of Gods *Messiah*" (882–3) brings about the War in Heaven and thus initiates the whole sequence of events comprising the action of the epic.

The next manifestation of the Son occurs on the third day of the War in Heaven, when he rides out in the chariot of his Father and drives the rebels before him like a herd of goats to the bottomless pit. As the Father points out, the action is designed to show the Son's power "above compare" (vi, 705), but the Son acknowledges the source of that power when he replies (vi, 734–6)

> I ... can put on
> Thy terrors, as I put thy mildness on,
> Image of thee in all things.

This negative expression of power is shortly balanced by a positive one, for in the Son's third appearance he acts as creator of the universe and of man. As the angel choir points out in the celebrations of the first sabbath, when all is complete, "to create / Is greater than created to destroy" (vii, 606–7).

More crucial to our impression of the Son than any of these early deeds, however, is his role as Mediator between God and man. His decision to become man's ransom and redeemer is presented dramatically in the council in Heaven in BOOK III, where the dialogue of Father and Son provides a full elaboration of the doctrine of atonement. After the Fall, we watch the Son begin his work for mankind as he descends to the garden, passes judgment on Adam and Eve, and then covers their inward nakedness with his robe of righteousness in order to protect them from "his Father's sight." (x, 223) Shortly after we see him once again in Heaven with his Father, making intercession for Adam and Eve and praying that his merit may be imputed to them. I shall have more to say about this role shortly, but it is worth noticing that he has already taken on his threefold office of prophet, priest, and king, the first in his prophecy concerning the seed of the woman which will bruise the serpent's head, the second in his priestly role as intercessor, and the third in his exercise of rule.[5] His work of redemption has in fact begun, although it is left to Michael, in his history of the world, to show how the Incarnation, Passion, and Death of Christ are to complete that work in the future.

The richness of the figure of the Son is due in part to the variety of his functions – we see him as destroyer and Creator, companion of the Father and restorer of mankind, a divine power of dazzling splendour and a humble minister to fallen man. Further significance, however, is provided by the range of attitudes taken toward the Son by the other characters. The Father always speaks of him as the beloved Son in whom he rests well pleased. Emphasis falls repeatedly on the way the Son deserves his high place at the right hand of the Father. At each of his appearances in Heaven he is illuminated by a blazing effulgence of glory, and one has the

5 Milton discusses the three offices in *De Doctrina Christiana*, *Works*, xv, 285 ff. See also Barbara K. Lewalski, *Milton's Brief Epic* (Brown University Press 1966), ch. vII.

sense that each new act of obedience increases his esteem in the eyes of his Father and consequently also increases his power. The climax to this progress, chronologically late but occurring at an early point in the poem, is the heavenly council at which the Son accepts the sad but heroic task of dying that man may live. By this act of self-sacrifice, the Father explains, he proves himself "By Merit more than Birthright Son of God, / Found worthiest to be so by being Good." (III, 309–10) It is now that he is told he will become universal king, and his new stature is celebrated by the angel choir when, having praised the Father, they comment on the divine love of the Son and vow that "thy Name / Shall be the copious matter of my Song / Henceforth, and never shall my Harp thy praise / Forget, nor from thy Fathers praise disjoin." (III, 412–15) In all this there is more than a hint of adoptianism. The Son seems to be involved, like all other creatures but the hopelessly lost, in a process of growth and education. The successive acts of obedience which from one point of view are the steps leading down to his humiliation in the form of man can also be seen as the stages by which he proves his title as Son of God.

Another feature of the Son's relation to the Father, one that is present in every scene in which he appears, is his subordinate position. I am not concerned at the moment with the vexed theological issues surrounding Milton's anti-Trinitarianism, but rather with the undeniable effect of the way in which the relations of Father and Son are presented. On almost every occasion in which the Son acts, power is transferred to him by the Father. As he goes out in the chariot of "Paternal Deitie" to quell the rebel angels, for example, we are told that he receives a transfusion of "Vertue and Grace / Immense" (VI, 703), and when he descends into the chaos to begin his work of creation, he is accompanied by the "overshadowing Spirit and might" (VII, 165) of the Father. Only in his voluntary abdication of power to become a ransom for man does this pattern seem broken, yet even here there is the assurance that the Father, who is the source of life, will not abandon him in the grave. Closely related to this theme of dependence are the many references to the idea that the Son expresses the Father. In *De Doctrina Christiana*, Milton observes that since the Son is the image of the Father, he cannot be identical with him (xiv, 401), and it is just such an implication which emerges from the poem. It is the Father who initiates action in speeches of unmatchable authority and self-assurance, while the Son reveals his perfect accord with the Father by the manner in which he manifests his will. Ultimately every divine act, even the mercy shown to man, finds its origin in the Father.

All the other figures of the poem are of course in a subordinate relation to the Son. But Satan and his followers refuse to recognize this fact, and as a consequence they speak as if the Son did not exist. Even before his expulsion from Heaven, Satan's bitterness is directed toward the Father and his unjust administration of power; after the expulsion, there is scarcely another reference to the Son by Satan, and not a single one which clearly distinguishes him from the Father.[6] It is beneath Satan's dignity, apparently, to engage in battle with anyone less than the supreme, nor can he admit that he suffered defeat at the hands of a rival for whom he professes contempt. He is in any case living out his own version of the role of Son of God. The Son is absent even from Satan's most retired and heart-felt meditations, and the point is obviously that for him there is no mediator, no hope, as he puts the matter in *Paradise Regained* (iii, 216–22), of interposing a cooling shade between himself and the wrath of God.

Another figure who does not need a mediator, at least in the sense of a ransom or an intercessor, is Raphael, but his self-sufficiency arises from the fact that he remains unfallen. Raphael's view of the Son, then, is one which befits a creature who has remained perfectly obedient to the divine will.

6 See C. A. Patrides, "The Godhead in *Paradise Lost*: Dogma or Drama," *JEGP*, LXIV (1965), 32.

It is thus particularly appropriate that the angel stresses the harmonious interplay of will between Father and Son. His account of the creation seems deliberately designed to prevent any simple separation of the functions of the divine actors. The Father, Raphael remarks, remained in Heaven during the creation, delegating the task to the Son: "by thee / This I perform, speak thou, and be it don." (VII, 163–4) Yet (such is the privilege of Omnipotence!) the Father also accompanied the Son invisibly, so that Raphael can speak of (VII, 208–9)

> The King of Glorie in his powerful Word
> And Spirit coming to create new Worlds.

The relationship is as close as that of speaker and word spoken, so that in one sense it is the Father who is the Creator, in another sense the Son. Raphael's account bears out the doctrine elaborated by Milton in his theological treatise that the Son is not the principal cause of the creation, nor a joint cause, but only an instrumental cause.[7] The unfallen angel, Raphael, understands the obedience of the subordinate being, and the harmony of will and aim which makes that obedience spontaneous and freely given.

Adam's view of the Son is difficult to define because it develops and changes. In the prelapsarian state he has no need of a redeemer or mediator. He is close to God, and holds frequent conversations with a divine presence or heavenly vision that visits him in the garden. Adam is a natural theologian, and he can see by the beauty and design of the universe that the power which made it must be infinitely good. When he is confronted by that power, or by a manifestation of it in something approximating human form, the only names he can find to call it are those of Author and Maker.

---

7 The Father is he "of whom ... from whom ... for whom ... through whom, and on account of whom are all things," while the Son is only he "by whom" they exist. *De Doctrina Christiana, Works,* XIV, 205.

The figure with whom he conducts his "celestial Colloquy" (VIII, 455) is undoubtedly the Son, but the Son acting as the voice of God and speaking on occasion words which are appropriate to the Father only.[8] One wonders what effect Raphael's revelation of the distinction between Father and Son would have had on Adam if he had remained in his unfallen state. No doubt Adam recognizes in the free service of the Father by the Son a model of his own filial relationship to God. But since he has no problems, he has no special need for the Son. With the Fall, all is changed. When the Son appears in the garden to pass sentence of death upon man, we are reminded of his earlier visits,[9] and this serves to throw into relief the fact that he now comes, not as formerly to relay the voice of God, but to provide a shield to protect man against the Father's wrath. He has commenced his work of mediation, although Adam will not become aware of the change and its implications until he has been instructed and illuminated by Michael. Ultimately Adam is brought to the realization that he will regain the liberty which was his before the Fall only through the offices of the Son.

Behind the portrayal of the Son in *Paradise Lost* lies Milton's examination of belief in his theological treatise, and particularly his exploration of the doctrines of the Trinity and the Incarnation. Thinking of this elaborate subject, one might feel a twinge of pity for those fallen angels who "reason'd high" with "thoughts more elevate" than their companions, but who "found no end, in wandring mazes lost." (II, 558–61) Recent criticism of Milton's views concerning the Son has brought a great deal of new and relevant information to bear on the subject, but it has done little to simplify it. The revision of critical attitudes toward Milton's theology of the Son was to a large extent initiated by the

8 "Seem I to thee sufficiently possest / Of happiness, or not? who am alone / From all Eternity, for none I know / Second to mee or like, equal much less." (VIII, 403–6)
9 See X, 103–4; 119–21.

appearance of several new studies of patristic thought, particularly by H. A. Wolfson's *Philosophy of the Church Fathers.*[10] In the light of Wolfson's study of patristic views concerning the Godhead, it has proved possible to reassess Milton's position. That it should be so is testimony to the comprehensiveness of those philological and historical studies by which Milton hoped to restore religion from "the corruptions of more than thirteen-hundred years." (*Works*, XIV, 3) His aim, shared by many of his contemporaries, was to press behind the formulations of the great councils of the third and fourth centuries to a simpler and less metaphysical theology, couched wherever possible in the very words of biblical revelation. Recent scholarship, drawing on the studies of Wolfson, G. L. Prestige, and others, has demonstrated how at point after point Milton's aim brings him close to the doctrines of such early Fathers as Tertullian and Origen, and to the subordinationism which was prevalent in the ante-Nicean period.[11]

Fortunately it is not necessary for us to reach a final conclusion about Milton's supposed Arianism. Those who believe the term is applicable to his rejection of the orthodox Trinity point out that he is like Arius in his denial of one

10 H. A. Wolfson, *Philosophy of the Church Fathers* (Harvard University Press 1956, revised edition 1964).

11 On this subject, see particularly the work of W. B. Hunter, "Milton's Arianism Reconsidered," *Harvard Theological Review*, LII (1959), 9–35; "The Meaning of 'Holy Light' in *Paradise Lost* III,"*MLN*, LXXIV (1959), 589–92; "Some Problems in John Milton's Theological Vocabulary," *Harvard Theological Review*, LVII (1964), 353–65. Hunter's views have been supported and elaborated by C. A. Patrides, "Milton and Arianism," *JHI*, XXV (1964), 423–9; *Milton and the Christian Tradition* (Oxford 1966), 15–22; and J. H. Adamson, "Milton's Arianism," *Harvard Theological Review*, LIV (1961), 269–76. Dissent has been voiced by Maurice Kelley, "Milton's Arianism Again Considered," *Harvard Theological Review*, LIII (1960) 195–205; John A. Clair, "A Note on Milton's 'Arianism'," in *Essays and Studies in Language and Literature*, ed. H. H. Petit (Pittsburg 1964); and Barbara Lewalski, *Milton's Brief Epic* (Brown University Press 1966), 133–63.

essence to the Father and the Son, in his insistence that the Son is not co-equal and co-eternal with the Father, and in his view that the Son was generated in time by a free act of the Father. Those who deny that the term is appropriate point out that Milton does not, like Arius, hold that the Son was created out of nothing, and they add that he gives the Son divine status by maintaining that he was made out of God's own substance. "God," Milton noted, "imparted to the Son as much as he pleased of the divine nature, nay of the divine substance itself. ..." (*Works*, xiv, 193) It is clear, I think, that if we give the term "Arian" a restricted definition, making it applicable only to those theologies which endorse all the main principles of Arius, then it can not be used to describe Milton's brand of anti-Trinitarianism. On the other hand, looking to the broader issues we find that Milton is close to the Arians in his denial of a completely unique status to the relations of Father and Son. True, he does not hold that the Son was created out of nothing. But then for Milton nothing can come from nothing, everything is made from matter which has been produced from the substance of God. Thus although his terms differ from those of the Arians, his emphasis is similar. Both diminish the uniqueness of the Son's generation[12] – the Arians, by saying that the Son, like the rest of the world, was created out of nothing, Milton by saying that the Son, like the rest of the world, was created out of God.[13]

12 On the importance of this uniqueness in patristic thought concerning the Son, see Wolfson, *Philosophy of the Church Fathers* (Harvard University Press 1964), 293 ff.

13 If "Arian" still seems too strong a term we might call Milton a "semi-Arian," drawing upon a definition provided by Alexander Ross: the semi-Arians, wrote Ross, "were those who neither would have Christ to be ... of the same individual essence with the Father ... nor yet of like essence ... but of a different essence [and] of a like will: and so they taught that Christ was not God in Essence, but in Will only, and operation." Πανσεβεια, *or, a View of all Religions in the World* (London 1653), 205.

One further point which should be made about Milton's attack on the traditional conception of the Trinity is the obvious centrality of the issue to his reform of dogma. Of all the other doctrinal issues in his theological work, only that of predestination has an equal importance. To the Son, Milton devotes the longest and most complex chapter in his treatise, a chapter which reiterates in every possible context the belief that Son and Father are one in will but not in essence or individual identity. He is perfectly well aware that he is flying in the face of orthodoxy, that he is espousing a doctrine not found in that creed which has at present "general acceptation." (*Works*, xiv, 177) It is this very awareness which drives him tirelessly forward in his argument. Why, one might ask, was the matter of such consuming importance to him? At least part of the answer is found in his belief that the doctrine of the Trinity is an insult to man's reason. The justification of God's ways to man is only possible if man is willing to think of God what is worthy of him. Milton's treatise is full of admonitions to think what is fitting, or suitable, or reasonable, of the Deity. In the doctrine of the Trinity he found the central example of perverse speculation, of "the deceitfulness of vain philosophy." (*Works*, xiv, 193) The advocates of the doctrine call it a mystery, he notes, but it is not so called in Scripture. It is, rather, a man-made mystery, a false mystery in which reason is used to establish a position contrary to reason. Rather than forming subtle imaginations about the drama of the three personalities in one Godhead, we should hold to the recognizable relationships between Father and Son which God has chosen to reveal to us. (*Works*, xiv, 197, 217; xv, 263) We should, that is, be content with the images and analogues, the ordinary forms of speech and thought, by which God has accommodated himself to our imaginations.

After the complexity of Milton's argument concerning the Trinity, his remarks on the doctrine of the Incarnation seem traditional and relatively straightforward. The Incarnate

Son, he explains, has a twofold nature, being both divine and human: "one ens, one person, is formed of [the] mutual hypostatic union of two natures or essences." (*Works*, xv, 271) The statement is in keeping with the orthodoxy established at the council of Chalcedon. It may seem surprising that Milton should reject with scorn the notion that there are three persons in one Godhead, and then accept without a qualm the doctrine that in Christ two natures unite in one being. The explanation, however, is not far to seek. The Incarnation is a true mystery, an event that surpasses the reach of man's reason, while the Trinity is a false mystery created by human ingenuity. The basis for such a distinction is found in Scripture, which speaks frequently of the mystery of the Incarnation, but never of the mystery of the Trinity. (*Works*, xv, 263) Thus he does not reduce the union of the two persons in Christ to an ethical and metaphoric union, as he might have done if he had followed Nestorian tradition.[14] The union is an ontological fact, a union of substances and not merely of wills. Since it is a mystery, however, "it behooves us to cease from devising subtle explanations, and to be contented with remaining wisely ignorant." (*Works*, xv, 273) Here, at the point where nature and supernature meet, Milton finds an event which defines the limits of human reason.

So far we have been examining Milton's views in the context provided by a much earlier period, as if he had been preparing a brief for the council of Nicea or of Chalcedon. In reality, of course, his reform of doctrine developed in response to the interplay of intellectual forces in his own period, and terms like Arianism and Nestorianism can apply to his views only loosely at best. Turning to the theology being written by Milton's contemporaries, we find that speculation about the Trinity is frequent and central. One of

14 The attempt to see Milton's view of Christ as Nestorian has been made by W. B. Hunter, "Milton on the Incarnation: Some More Heresies," *JHI*, xxi (1960), 349–69.

the most intellectually distinguished schools of thought to reveal such a preoccupation is that of the Cambridge Platonists, and recent criticism, emphasizing Milton's affinities with the Cambridge school, urges that he must to some degree be included in the group.[15] This is certainly true if we have in mind the ethical emphasis that runs through the writings of the group, but the Trinitarian speculations of men like Henry More and Ralph Cudworth are another matter altogether. Both these philosophers set out to reveal a correlation between the Christian Trinity and the Trinity of the Neo-Platonists. Their aim is to prove that the truths of Christian revelation were accessible, although in a dark and confused manner, to natural theologians who were unaware of Christianity. Such a correlation, they felt, would secure the doctrine of the Trinity from the charge of irrationality. But both writers are also attracted by the element of subordinationism in the Trinity of the pagan philosophers, and they agree that the crucial passages concerning the Son in the Athanasian creed should be interpreted generously in order to permit the Christian Platonist to retain an element of subordinationism.[16]

Superficially, their aim has something in common with Milton's, and it is obviously important that such speculation was in progress at Cambridge during the period. But it is a mistake, I think, to find in the work of these Platonists a very close parallel to Milton's views. In the first place, the Neo-Platonic conception of the necessary and eternal emanation of the second person from the first, and of the third from the second, is quite unlike Milton's creationist view. For Milton, the Son was created at a particular time by an act of volition on the part of the Father. The whole thrust of his interpretation supports the importance of will in the divine

15 See Hunter, "Milton's Arianism Reconsidered," 32, 35.
16 Ralph Cudworth, The True Intellectual System of the Universe (London 1678), 606 ff., and Henry More, An Explanation of the Grand Mystery of Godliness (London 1660), 456.

economy. Not only is there no trace of the Neo-Platonic One-Soul-Mind terminology in his discussion, but he is even chary of employing the traditional Logos terminology in connection with the Son.

Secondly, Milton would never appeal to the philosophers in a matter of this kind. It is particularly instructive to consider the gap which separates his view of this subject from that of Henry More. The core of their differences can be found in their contrasting attitudes towards mystery. While Milton was bringing his treatise on Christian doctrine to fulfilment, More was writing *An Explanation of the Grand Mystery of Godliness*, a work which contains a sustained plea for the reinstatement of the concept of mystery in theology. More takes his stand in opposition to the kind of rationalism and biblicism represented by the Socinians. His theme is that "perpetual expectation" arouses wonder and respect. What does it matter, he asks,

> if the bottom of the Well be fathomless, if the Water we reach be but pure and useful? ... those that contend for an *absolute plainess and clearness in all parts of Religion*, shew more of clownishness ... then of wit ... they [take] it very ill that anything in The Mysterie of Godliness should be so *mysterious*, as that their conceited *Reason* should not be able to comprehend it.[17]

The whole emphasis here is alien to Milton, who accepts in a fairly extreme form the Protestant dictum that the Scripture is plain and perspicuous in all things necessary to salvation.[18] In More's view, however, the very lack of

17 More, *Mystery of Godliness*, 454.
18 More asks of his opponents (*Mystery of Godliness*, 454), "By what faculty can they demonstrate, that the Divine Oracles should mention nothing to us but what is the adequate object of our understandings?" Milton might well have answered in the words of the Son in *Paradise Regained* (1, 460–4): "God hath now sent his living Oracle / Into the World to teach his final will ... an inward Oracle / To all truth requisite for men to know."

definition is stimulating. The Christian philosopher "conceives a peculiar pleasure" in the "confused divination or obscure representation of things."[19] He becomes an initiate, penetrating ever further into an intelligible but inexhaustible mystery, finding spiritual nourishment in the very process of learning. And chief among the great inexhaustible mysteries are the doctrines of "the Triunity of the Godhead" and "the Divinity of Christ."[20] More's approach, then, presents a paradigm of those methods which Milton rejects. His love of mysteries is representative of the kind of gnosticism that Milton resists at every turn, and that he seeks to eliminate by his doctrine that God accommodates his truth to the imagination of man. Mysteries, Milton implies, are never fit subjects for meditation: thus, as we have seen, the Trinity is a false, man-made mystery, while the Incarnation, precisely because it is a true mystery, is forbidden as a subject of speculation.

There is little doubt that when More chastised those who seek "absolute plainess and clearness" in religion he had in mind the Socinians, and it is probable that he was thinking of the most prominent of the English Socinians, John Biddle. Biddle's attitude to mysteries is quite uncompromising, and strongly reminiscent of Milton's. He considers the false mystery of the Trinity an error which endangers the whole structure of reformed doctrine. Turning the tables on More, he argues that the Trinity is a pagan mystery which was produced by the influence of the Platonic philosophers on the early church. The council of Nicea, he maintains, was "beholding to the Platonists" for the notion of the co-essentiality of the three persons of the Trinity, and for overlaying the simple meaning of the gospel with high and witty notions that obscure the true humanity of Christ.[21]

19 More, *Mystery of Godliness*, 453.
20 *Ibid.*, 454.
21 *The Apostolical and True Opinion concerning the Holy Trinity* ... (London 1653), 85.

Henry More is singled out by Biddle for particular criticism as an example of the kind of Platonist who scorns the plain and certain word of God in favour of mystical interpretations.[22]

Milton, I suggest, is much closer in his views to the Socinianism of Biddle than to the Platonism of More. The whole tenor of Biddle's approach to the mystery of the Trinity, with his unflagging determination to "assert nothing ... but onely introduce the Scripture faithfully uttering its own assertions,"[23] is reminiscent of Milton. The attempt to associate Milton with Socinianism has been criticized on the ground that the Socinians were "relatively unimportant writers who never achieved any real intellectual leadership."[24] But such a view does not take into account the pervasiveness of Socinian ideas in the period, the influence which such ideas exerted over writers who sympathized but were not converts, and the prestige lent to the movement by the scholarship of its continental exponents. Biddle himself was a school teacher, a humanist, and a man prepared to suffer with patience for his beliefs, and Milton could hardly have failed to sympathize with him. Attempts to show the direct influence of particular Socinian writers on Milton have proved inconclusive;[25] but there can be little doubt, I think, that the movement exercised a profound and lasting influence upon him.

During his Italian journey Milton paused at Sienna, where Faustus Socinus was born a century earlier. It would not be surprising if during those conversations with "many persons of rank and learning" in Florence, there was mention of the Siennese nobleman whose sect was now flooding Europe

22 *A Twofold Catechism* ... (London 1654), c, 1v.
23 *Ibid.*, A, 4r.
24 W. B. Hunter, "Milton's Arianism Reconsidered," 14.
25 See, for example, M. A. Larson, "Milton and Servetus: A Study of Sources of his Theology," *PMLA,* xli (1926), 891–934; Louis A. Wood, *The Form and Origin of Milton's Antitrinitarian Conception* (London, Ontario 1911).

with literature. It was on the same journey, it is worth remembering, that he met "the learned Hugo Grotius," whose liberal theology caused him to be repeatedly associated with Socinianism.[26] Although the exact point at which Milton became aware of Socinianism is in doubt, definite evidence exists to prove that by 1650 he had come into contact with the seminal work of the movement in England, the *Racovian Catechism*, which was reissued in a Latin edition in 1651, and in a free English translation, almost certainly by Biddle, in 1652.[27] His familiarity with Socinian attitudes is evident throughout his theological treatise,[28] and it appears probable that he included them among those "heretics, so called" whose views, he maintains, are frequently closer to the truth of Scripture than are the views of those considered orthodox. (*Works*, XIV, 15)

There was good reason for Milton's interest in the Socinians. They, too, were constructing a theodicy and justifying God's ways to men. They, too, developed doctrine in re-

26 *Defensio Secunda*, VIII, 123.
27 On the history of the *Racovian Catechism*, see H. John McLachlan, *Socinianism in Seventeenth-Century England* (Oxford 1951), and L. M. Oliver, *Harvard Library Bulletin*, VII (1953), 119–21. For Milton's mysterious but significant connection with the work, see J. M. French, *Life Records of John Milton*, under the following dates: 10 Aug. 1650; 27 Jan. 1652; 5 March 1652; 2 April 1652; and the addition in V, 421.
28 The extent of Milton's familiarity with Socinianism is suggested by his use of a work by Josue De La Place (Placaeus of Saumur), a French theologian who was an opponent of the Socinian movement. In a treatise called *Disputationes de Testimoniis et Argumentis e Veteri Testamento Petitis* ... (1651), La Place draws upon contemporary debates and attempts to demonstrate that the doctrine of the Trinity is supported by passages in the Old Testament. Milton, in his discussion of those who "revert from the gospel to the times of the law" in order to maintain the co-essentiality of Father and Son, attacks several of the arguments put forward by La Place. He names his opponent three times and quotes directly from his work. ("De Doctrina Christiana," *Works*, XIV, 277 ff.) We thus find Milton consciously aligning himself with the Socinians in his attack on Trinitarian dogma.

sponse to a double pressure – the demand that it be scriptural, and the demand that it be rational. Passing from Milton's *De Doctrina Christiana* to the *Racovian Catechism* of the Socinians, one experiences a shock of recognition. Not only is their approach to the Bible very similar to Milton's, but they are like him in their frequent admonitions to think of God what is morally worthy of him. It is not surprising, then, that both works give prominence to the same doctrines, and especially to those concerned with the nature of Christ. Yet when we turn to particular issues, the gulf which separates Milton from the Socinians becomes increasingly evident.

The principle which informs Socinian theology is that of combating the Calvinist emphasis on grace, with its corollaries of predestination and saving faith. Their revision of doctrine leads them into three main areas of controversy. First, they reject the doctrine of the Trinity. The *Catechism* maintains, as does Milton, that this doctrine is both unscriptural and contrary to reason.[29] Secondly, they reject the doctrine of the pre-existence of the Son. Christ, they argue, was the "first born of every creature" only in the sense that he was the first man to be made new under the gospel. He was, indeed, fully human, possessing neither divine power nor divine knowledge in himself, and whatever supernatural qualities he revealed in his acts were received as a gift from the Father.[30] Basically, then, the Socinian treatise urges the heresy known as Ebionism or Photinism: Christ was an unusually good man who received divine favour because of his merit. His chief function is exemplary.

This attack on the idea of Christ's divinity, however, leads on to a third major departure from orthodoxy. Protestant thought concerning the atonement made by Christ had become unusually rigid, inflexible, and uniform. From

29 See *The Racovian Catechism*, trans. Thomas Rees (London 1818), 45.
30 *The Racovian Catechism*, section IV, ch. I.

Luther and Calvin to Ussher and Lancelot Andrewes, Protestant theologians insisted on interpreting the atonement in terms of the doctrine of satisfaction.[31] Man, it was held, is incapable of making expiation for sin, and for this reason the Son of God became his substitute and paid the penalty which he had incurred. In his death, Christ bore the punishment due to man's sin, and consequently satisfied divine justice. The Socinian aims find their fullest realization in the rejection of this satisfaction doctrine. It is, they argued, a doctrine which presents an unworthy picture of God, for it shows him unable to freely forgive sin and it introduces an absurd conflict between his attributes of justice and mercy. Moreover, the doctrine takes away the motive for moral action. If the satisfaction made by Christ is perfect, then man need not contribute anything. Indolence may go hand in hand with virtue. Thus their argument ends by urging that men should imitate Christ, rather than rely on his imputed merit.

Milton's theology, I believe, was shaped to a significant extent by his response to Socinian thought. The movement must have held for him the value of a touchstone for theology which is oriented toward man, and which places the primary emphasis on human values. He used it, perhaps, as a counterpoise for Calvinism, with its emphasis on faith and on grace. The humane God of the Socinians acted as a foil to the awesome Deity of the Calvinists. Yet Milton was quite deliberately avoiding both extremes, and as he on one hand revised and modified Calvinist doctrine, so, on the other, he distinguished his view at point after point from that of the Socinians.

With the Socinian rejection of the concept of a Trinity he is in general agreement, and much of the detail of his argu-

---

31 See C. A. Patrides, "Milton and the Protestant Theory of the Atonement," PMLA, LXXIV (1959), 7–13, and L. W. Grensted, A Short History of the Doctrine of the Atonement (Manchester 1920).

ment finds a close parallel in the *Catechism*. But he has no
sympathy with their conception of the Son: "certain it is,"
he writes, "whatever some moderns may allege to the con-
trary, that the Son existed in the beginning, under the name
of logos or word, and was the first of the whole creation, by
whom afterwards all other things were made." (*Works*, xiv,
181) He is careful to make it clear that the biblical phrase
"the first born of every creature" refers to the first being
created by God, and he mocks the subtleties of those who
seek to deny the pre-existence of the Son in order to maintain
his "purely human nature." (*Works*, xv, 263) That pre-
existent Son, moreover, possesses in Milton's view a share
of divine substance, and when he becomes incarnate his
nature is twofold, both divine and human. At every stage
Milton is deliberately excluding the Socinian position, and
embracing the view they characterize as Arian.[32]

It is in his handling of the doctrine of Christ's satisfaction,
however, that Milton takes the greatest pains to distinguish
himself from the Socinians. He clearly has them in mind
when he writes of those who, evading the evidence of
Scripture, "maintain that Christ dies, not in our stead, and
for our redemption, but merely for our advantage in the
abstract, and as an example to mankind." (*Works*, xv, 317–
19)[33] His own position, set forth both in poetry and prose,
was perfectly orthodox. As the Father explains during the

32 "... that the Lord Jesus was the first of the things made in the old
  creation, even our opponents cannot admit, unless they would
  become Arians. They must therefore grant that he is one, and
  indeed the first, among the productions of the new creation." *The
  Racovian Catechism*, trans. Thomas Rees (London 1818), 136–7.
33 Milton's rejection of the Socinian doctrine extends to details of
  argument. When he explains that the Greek expressions for "ran-
  som" employed in the New Testament "clearly denote the substi-
  tution of one person in place of another," he is deliberately ruling
  out the Socinian view that "ransom" is a highly metaphoric and
  rather vague term, and when he remarks that Christ's death pays
  the required price "for, that is to say, instead of," all mankind,
  he undoubtedly has in mind the Socinian claim that Christ dies,
  not instead of, but on account of, mankind.

council in Heaven in BOOK III of *Paradise Lost*, Adam and his whole posterity must die as a result of the Fall (210–12),

> Dye hee or Justice must; unless for him
> Som other able, and as willing, pay
> The rigid satisfaction, death for death.

The entire council, indeed, rises to a climax in the revelation of the Son's role as ransom, and one cannot escape the conclusion that this was a doctrine of peculiar importance to the poet.

I have tried to suggest how Milton's views on the Son were developed within the context provided by contemporary speculation and dogma. Like the Socinians, he turned away from the gnosticism which finds in the theological mysteries of religion an esoteric subject for devotion and meditation. He agreed with them, moreover, that religion should be based on the Bible and on reason, and that it should provide an image of God that is in harmony with the highest ethical ideals and practices. Yet he was not prepared to follow them in their depreciation of the supernatural elements in religion and their exclusive emphasis on ethical doctrine. Against these views he maintained the pre-existence of the Son, the dual nature of the Incarnate Christ, and the doctrine of Satisfaction.

Following the course of Milton's reaction against the Socinian theology, we might be tempted to feel that he has, at least temporarily, abandoned his effort to rationalize the theology of the Son. His legalistic formulation of the Satisfaction doctrine seems in particular to be at odds with the spirit of theodicy. The necessary sacrifice of the Son draws attention to something in the Father which is difficult to assess in terms of man's principles and rules, and the conflict of justice and mercy cannot be easily placed within a framework of purely human values. The Son's redemptive act is in any case an act which man cannot imitate; whereas it reconciles God to man, it also emphasizes man's helplessness, his inability to atone for sin, his dependence on grace.

There is, however, another side to Milton's argument, for the Son is seen as a true mediator who exercises his influence on man as well as on God. Throughout *De Doctrina Christiana*, Milton consistently envisages the Son's mediation as involving two main objects. The first, as we have seen, is the reconciliation of God to man, and this the Son accomplishes by fulfilling the law and paying the required price. His second object is the renovation of man, "that we may be conformed to the image of Christ, as well in his state of humiliation as of exaltation." (*Works*, xv, 333) Regeneration is thus a process both external and internal. Externally, it takes the form of justification – because of the satisfaction made by Christ, his merit is imputed to man through faith. Internally, it takes the form of the restoration of the image of God in the believer. The understanding is restored in great part to its primitive clearness, and the will to its primitive liberty, by the new spiritual life in Christ. (*Works*, xvi, 5)[34] This distinction, handled with the greatest care by Milton throughout his treatise, enables him to describe the Son both as an outward Saviour and as an inward principle of new life.

Once again, Whichcote's language provides the best possible commentary. Christ, Whichcote argues, is both an advocate for man, and a principle of grace within him. Those men flatter themselves, he writes "who thinke of reconciliation with God, by meanes of a Saviour acting upon God in their behalfe; and not also working in or upon them, to make them God-like."[35] Both aspects of the work of Christ are important, but the first, his satisfaction for man's sins, is something that can be known once and for all by a

---

34 On the importance of this idea in Milton's theology, see Arthur Barker, *Milton and the Puritan Dilemma* (University of Toronto Press 1942), ch. xvii, as well as his essay in the present collection.

35 *Moral and religious aphorisms ... to which are added eight letters which passed between Dr. Whichcote and Dr. Tuckney*, ed. Samuel Salter (London 1753), 75.

"thorowe consideration," while the second, man's transformation into the "spirit, image and nature" of Christ, is a continuing process within each individual.[36] In much the same way, Milton preserves the distinction between the formal doctrine of satisfaction and the inward realization of Christ. The Son of God, he would have agreed, is "a principle of divine life within us, as well as a saviour without us."[37]

If we return, briefly, to Milton's epic, we can see how the figure of the Son in the poem is consistent with the principles of his theodicy. The heaven which Milton there depicts holds little for the gnostic lover of mysteries. It is not likely to arouse the "peculiar pleasure" which can be derived, according to Henry More, from the "confused divination or obscure representation of things." There is, of course, an element of real mystery in the heaven of *Paradise Lost*, and it is nowhere more evident than in the use of imagery of light. Yet the reader is not invited to linger over that divine presence which is "Dark with excessive bright" (III, 380), nor is he enticed by symbol, myth, or ritual to believe that he is exploring the mystery of God's identity. Instead, the poem presents him with dramatic dialogue, and with a God who is quite clearly asking "Are not my ways equal?" and thus inviting man to test the justice of his ways by man's own principles and rules. He is a God, then, who is eager to accommodate himself to man's understanding, and to present his purpose in a manner which is meaningful within the framework of human values. Thus, as we saw, the relations of Father and Son are developed in terms which emphasize unity of will and separateness of identity. Since the Son is a subordinate being, Milton is able to express the drama of his relationship with the Father in a fashion which is ethical rather than metaphysical; the chief mystery of that relationship lies in the harmony which turns obedience into perfect freedom.

36 *Ibid.*, 125.   37 *Ibid.*

Yet Milton is far from implying that these divine beings function in a merely exemplary fashion. In accommodating himself to man's understanding, God also makes clear the limits and inadequacies of that understanding. The Father is unknowable in himself, being made manifest only through the Son, while the Son also possesses powers which are beyond the reach of man, not merely supernatural powers of creation and destruction, but more than human virtues of love and obedience. The drama of his relation with the Father culminates in the Incarnation, an event in itself beyond the capacities of man to fully understand. Although the Incarnation does not actually occur within the time span of the action in Milton's epic, it is nonetheless anticipated and foreshadowed, so that we are aware of it as the destination toward which the events of the poem are all-moving. In thus insisting on the continuity between the pre-existent Son and the Incarnate Son, Milton makes his story embody his objections to Socinianism, while his doctrine of Satisfaction is a more specific way of opposing the kind of moral activism found in the Socinian ethic.

The key to Milton's thought about the Son of God is thus to be found in his conception of the Son's office of mediator. The Son cannot be the same as the Father, for then he would be acting as a mediator to himself; yet he cannot be merely human, or he would lack the power to redeem man from bondage and to restore his freedom and understanding. He must, then, hold an intermediate position, a position between the absolute Deity and mankind, if he is to perform his office. Thus, as we have seen, Milton rejects the orthodox conception of the Trinity and yet with equal vigour turns away from the Socinian alternative.

As I have tried to suggest, this conception of the Son as mediator is prominent in *Paradise Lost*. It remains to ask whether the poem, like the treatise, presents his office in terms of two main functions, one external, the other internal, one the priestly work of satisfaction, the other the prophetic work of illumination. The answer, I believe, is that this distinction is present at several points in the poem, and that it is established, not merely through overt, doctrinal statement, but more subtly in terms of character and dramatic situation.

One powerful example of this complex pattern will have to suffice. The conception of atonement we have been exploring can be seen operating through the great soliloquy in which Adam expresses his bitterness and despair after the Fall. In that speech, you will remember, Adam meditates on the various possible meanings of the sentence of death which has been passed upon him, each new possibility worse than the last, and these thoughts draw him into questioning the ways of God. He would like to find some justification for himself, a strategy for turning the blame back on his Creator, yet in the end he realizes that all his arguments are mere excuses. With mounting terror, he acknowledges that God is just and that there is no way in which that justice can be satisfied. The soliloquy rises to an agony of fear and self-reproach: (x, 828–41)

> Him after all Disputes
> Forc't I absolve: all my evasions vain
> And reasonings, though through Mazes, lead me still
> But to my own conviction: first and last
> On mee, mee onely, as the sourse and spring
> Of all corruption, all the blame lights due;
> So might the wrauth. Fond wish! couldst thou support
> That burden heavier than the Earth to bear,
> Then all the World much heavier, though divided
> With that bad Woman? Thus what thou desir'st
> And what thou fearst, alike destroyes all hope
> Of refuge, and concludes thee miserable
> Beyond all past example and future,
> To *Satan* only like both crime and doom.

Adam is unable to save himself. He has reached the end of his resources, and he realizes that he is powerless to change the situation. He gropes toward the idea of atonement, yet despairingly, because he knows himself incapable of bearing the weight of God's wrath, that burden heavier than the earth. Thus Milton has managed to combine a moment of tragic intensity with the doctrine that man can be saved only by the righteousness of Christ. At the same time, however, Adam's humility and self-reproach point the way to his repentance, and thus to the restoration of the image of God within him. Already God's grace, operating through the Son, has begun the work of regeneration.

Both themes – justification and inward regeneration – are developed further in the events which follow, and are then brought to fulfilment during Michael's visit to Adam. In order to complete Adam's education, Michael presents to him the future history of the world. It is on the whole a depressing spectacle, a futile cycle which demonstrates, in a wide variety of situations, the spiritual bankruptcy of man. However, it also manifests God's plan for the salvation of man, a plan which finally culminates in the life and death of Christ, who by his obedience releases man from the power of Satan. Sin, Michael explains to Adam, will never "hurt them more who rightly trust / In this his satisfaction." (XII, 418–19) Adam now understands how the Son will act as man's ransom. At the same time, however, he has been educated concerning the nature of moral action in a fallen world. He has been shown the saints, and also the God-man whom the saints all typify. The Incarnate Son now appears as the ultimate pattern of obedience and love, as Adam recognizes when he says that he has been taught true heroism "by his example whom I now / Acknowledge my Redeemer ever blest." (XII, 573–4) In Whichcote's language, Christ has proved "a principle of grace" within Adam, as well as an "advocate" for him. As Milton had argued many years before, in an early and unfinished poem, the Son is a "Most perfect *Hero*, tried in heaviest plight / Of labors huge and hard, too hard for human wight."

"PARADISE LOST"

The Web of Responsibility

BALACHANDRA RAJAN

When Raleigh contemplates the crisis of *Paradise Lost* he says decisively that "there is not an incident, hardly a line of the poem, but leads backwards or forwards to those central lines of the Ninth Book." The "central lines" are those which recount Eve's plucking and eating of the apple. "From this point," Raleigh continues, "radiates a plot so immense in scope, that the history of the world from the first preaching of the Gospel to the Millennium occupies only some fifty lines of Milton's Epilogue."[1] When Tillyard disagrees with Raleigh on the location of the crisis he directs our attention to Adam's and Eve's repentance. "The whole elaborate edifice," he says, "has been staged to give all possible weight to a quite uncomplicated and commonplace trickle of pure human sympathy, the first touch of regeneration, a small

1 Walter Raleigh, *Milton* (London 1915), 81–2.

beginning but stronger than the pretensions of satanic in-
genuity, like some faint flow of pale, clear oil issuing from a
huge and grotesquely carved oil-press; all this complication
of apparatus just for *that*."[2] It is possible to have different
views of where the crisis of *Paradise Lost* occurs.[3] It is also
possible to believe that there is more than one crisis or to
conclude, as Tillyard himself suggests,[4] that we should think
not of a point but of an area of crisis. Most persuasive per-
haps is the view of G. A. Wilkes that the search for a crisis
results in misreading the poem.[5] For the time being we must
refrain from committing ourselves to any of these fascinat-
ing and distracting alternatives. Rather, we must concen-
trate on what is suggested both by Raleigh's characteristic
clarity and by that uncharacteristic flurry of excitement that
invades Tillyard's normally bland prose. The two scholars
disagree on what constitutes the crucial act of choice but
they agree on the minuteness of the act and on the huge
hinterland of motivation and consequence which converges
on the act and radiates from it. Both accept the vast design[6]
and the vulnerable centre, the enormous pressures that are
brought to bear on the enclosed moment in the walled-in
garden.

As the times change the conditions of wisdom alter and
what was once indisputable as a pattern of truth becomes
only accessible as a metaphoric structure. It is not always
easy to maintain that on the 22nd of April in 4004 BC, an

2 E. M. W. Tillyard, *Studies in Milton* (London 1951), 43.
3 See in particular, Millicent Bell, "The Fallacy of the Fall in *Para-
   dise Lost*," *PMLA*, LXVIII (1953), 863–83, and H. V. S. Ogden "The
   Crisis of *Paradise Lost* Reconsidered," *PQ*, XXXVI (1957), 1–19.
4 Tillyard, *Studies in Milton*, 13–14.
5 G. A. Wilkes, *The Thesis of "Paradise Lost"* (Melbourne 1961).
   Wilkes observes (p. 42) that "The weight of Milton's conception
   is not poised on one episode analysed by Professor Waldock or on
   another singled out by Dr. Tillyard: its weight is distributed
   through the whole structure and all twelve books of the poem help
   to support it."
6 Marvell's phrase has been used as the title of a recent book on
   Yeats.

apple eaten in Mesopotamia where apples do not normally grow, accounts for a decisive failure in ourselves. What we are dealing with is a fable of the human condition: indeed three hundred years of the reading of *Paradise Lost* entitle us to make use of the word "myth." This myth is sometimes described as a myth of radical evil: in other words it invokes the recognition that we are to some degree imprisoned in ourselves, that liberation can only follow on moral transformation and that transformation depends on our spontaneous dependence on a power beyond ourselves which restores to us the freedom of our proper place in reality. The last books of *Paradise Lost* powerfully convey this recognition both through the manner in which the trickle of sin broadens into the torrent of history and through the manner in which the seed of repentance grows into the harvest of redemption. But the last two books are only a sixth of *Paradise Lost* and it has required some effort by Milton scholars to show that they are organically part of the epic and not simply the despairing postscript of a defeated reformer. Radical evil has its place in the web of *Paradise Lost* but the web itself is perhaps better explored by other guiding principles such as infinite responsibility and the great movements of meaning and consequence that are made to centre round the gift of freedom.[7]

That *Paradise Lost* is the only poem to present the celestial cycle in its entirety has been recognized,[8] but due attention has not always been given to Milton's shaping of the cycle. The typical chronology maintained that the angels were created with the world and fell during the creation. Milton's view that the angels fell before the world was created was not without precedent but it was not the view of his time.[9]

7   See Kester Svendsen, "*Paradise Lost* as Alternative," *Humanities Association Bulletin*, xviii (1967), 35–42. Professor Svendsen's article appeared after this paper was written.

8   Watson Kirkconnell, *The Celestial Cycle* (Toronto 1952), Intro., xxii.

9   *Paradise Lost and the Seventeenth Century Reader*, 35 and 145, n. 10.

We know from the *De Doctrina*[10] that he believed in his account of events, but *Paradise Lost* obliges us to look not so much at what Milton believed as what he made of what he believed in or invented. When both the true and the feigned seem to point to the same aesthetic purpose we can be slightly more confident that we are right in our sense of the purpose. To return to the celestial cycle, Milton's more spacious planning enables him to set apart human and heavenly history, to suggest more clearly how history repeats itself, to link the fall of Satan with that of Adam and Eve, and to link the creation with the Atonement. The rhythm of light out of darkness which is thereby established becomes not simply an assertion of the ways of providence but part of the poem's basic symmetry. The great confrontations of the epic have already been drawn and the shape they compose is seen as the pattern of time.

Milton's shaping of a work has always a deep creative consistency. All that he does is finely responsive to a controlling logic, putting around that logic the power and sweep of the poem. If he achieves certain results in his treatment of time, he achieves them again in his interpretation of space. In both dimensions the field of organization is the theoretical maximum and comprehensiveness becomes an aesthetic virtue because all things in that comprehensiveness are mobilized, interconnected, and set meaningfully within an order of things the pivot of which is man's nature and his destiny.

Milton's universe is usually described as Ptolemaic; it is so only within what is hesitantly termed the hard outer shell of the created world.[11] The chaos which rages against the world is by no means the first matter of the *De Doctrina*[12] and while taking up hints and guesses from Lucretius,

11 Allan H. Gilbert, "The Outside Shell of Milton's World," *SP*, xx
10 *Works*, xv, 33–5.
    (1923), 444–7; Harry F. Robins, "The Unnecessary Shell of Milton's World," *Studies in Honour of T. W. Baldwin*, ed. D. C. Allen (Urbana 1958), 211–19.
12 A. S. P. Woodhouse, "Notes on Milton's Views on the Creation: The Initial Phase," *PQ*, xxviii (1949), 211–36 and esp. 229, n. 30.

Spenser, and elsewhere, remains impressively Milton's own creation.[13] Ontologically, the world is a short "walk" from chaos, to use a phrase by the "Anarch old" which is both unexpectedly and arrestingly casual. It is hung from heaven by a golden chain which links classical precedents with Mediaeval and Renaissance ideas of harmony; but it is also joined to hell by a causeway which Milton's imagination built, even though its diabolic span encompasses scriptural and Virgilian texts. The decisions which confront man become all the more momentous when they are affirmed so insistently in the symbols of his universe.

God's eminence is "dark with excessive bright." Chaos is "Darkness profound" and hell "darkness visible." (III, 380; VII, 233; I, 63) These discriminations are expressive of an alert poetic intelligence able not only to proclaim but to populate a universe, taking up the literary past when it can, but also ignoring it when it must. If chaos is Milton's creation, hell is its perversely disciplined enclave, an anti-world carved destructively out of the non-world. Milton's location of hell is like his chronology, his own imaginative decision, taken tellingly against the weight of precedent.[14] In placing it "As far remov'd from God and light of Heav'n / As from the Center thrice to th' utmost Pole" (I, 73–4), he is expecting us to appreciate his talent in the solemn game of outdoing Virgil and Homer but also to recognize that there is more serious business on hand. Spatial distance from the light can also be moral distance, "Glory obscur'd" is on the way to "Darkness visible," and "fardest from him is best" is meant to be heard as a cry not only of heroic defiance but of ultimate alienation.[15] The mind as its own place becomes "my-

13 Walter C. Curry, Milton's *Ontology, Cosmogony, and Physics* (Lexington 1957), 48–91; A. B. Chambers, "Chaos in *Paradise Lost*," *JHI*, XXIV (1963), 55–84.

14 The *De Doctrina* (*Works*, XV, 373–5) restricts its claim of support to Luther, Chrysostom, and "some later divines."

15 *PL*, I, 593–4; I, 247. See also I, 97; IV, 835–51. The reverse of this process can be found in the *Paradiso* where Beatrice becomes more and more beautiful as she rises to the ultimate light.

self am Hell"; the mind opened to God can become the para-
dise within. It is scarcely necessary to multiply examples;
the principle is central and the reader should not be deprived
of the pleasure of discovering and connecting its detailed
manifestations.

As we read *Paradise Lost* we become more and more aware
of the steady mobilization of what Blake and Yeats would
call contraries: light and darkness, good and evil, reason and
passion, creation and destruction, supernal grace and sinful-
ness. Each set of contraries evokes the others and is reflected
into them, so that as we advance through the poem, we be-
come conscious of a web of interconnectedness, steadily
growing in its controlled complexity. The location of hell
now takes its place in the poem, as everything does if we look
for the place with patience. The purpose is to build into the
cosmography of the poem our sense of the poem's massed
polarities. The two armies under their creative and destruc-
tive Trinities confront each other across the created universe
and like chaos beating upon the walls of that universe, the
force of inescapable cosmic issues presses steadily upon the
fragile peace of Paradise.

In a poem of the scope of *Paradise Lost*, oppositions of
concept and imagery are not enough. A narrative poem must
encompass and move through a series of dramatic opposi-
tions. Few things in *Paradise Lost* are more striking than the
manner in which Milton pushes satire almost to the edge of
blasphemy in underlining his contrast between the divine
and satanic trinities. The two councils, infernal and celestial,
play their part in this differentiation. Twenty years ago it
might have been necessary to insist on the results made
possible by this uniquely inclusive and dramatic structure.
In the present state of scholarship such underlining is no
longer required. But gains can seldom be made without
paying a price; the price paid here is that a contemplative
heaven must be renounced and that the divine must be
disclosed in action rather than through its reflected radiance
in things. Laments that Milton did not provide us with a

Dantesque heaven are fairly frequent; these laments fail to recognize that poets, like men of affairs, have only limited options and that to choose one option is to decide against others.[16] Moreover, the choice of an option is a choice decisive for the whole poem, assuming that the poem has some degree of integrity; what we discuss in seminars as the problem of Heaven cannot be treated as the problem of Heaven alone.

In the contrast between the two trinities Milton makes it clear that he knows what he wants to do and that, like all artists who have felt within themselves the rights of their own poetry, he is prepared to run certain imaginative risks to do it. His design may not be the best of all possible designs, though those who feel this should ask themselves about the total and not merely the local alternatives. But Milton's sense of the design is consistent and decisive. In his presentation of Christ as much as in his treatment of the two trinities, Milton shows his desire to give dramatic substance and animation to the oppositions of imagery and concept that extend and ramify through the poem. The web of responsibility proliferates and yet draws together; and the movement from mind to cosmos and from cosmos to mind, so characteristic of the fluency of the epic, bears with elaborated weight on the basic contentions within the nature of man.

It is unfortunate that in discussing what is unusual about Christ we should limit ourselves to a discussion of theology. Arianism or Subordinationism is not Milton's only way of being original. There are perhaps four occasions on which Milton's presentation of Christ departs from tradition. Three of these at least, have little to do with Subordinationism; but

16 Milton had an important precedent for his presentation of Heaven in Tasso but even if he had not read Davenant's *Preface to Gondibert* he could not have been oblivious to the kind of objection that Davenant urges against Tasso's presentation. See *Critical Essays of the Seventeenth Century*, ed. J. D. Spingarn (Oxford 1908), II, 5.

all four of them have much to do with the poem. Though
there is a well-established practice of having Truth, Justice,
Peace, and Mercy consider man's fate before the throne of
God, this constitutes no real precedent for a dialogue be-
tween two persons of the Trinity.[17] A true precedent is by
no means easy to find. Again, Milton's treatment of the
Battle in Heaven departs from typical interpretations of the
Book of *Revelation* for as Milton himself points out, "it is
generally supposed that Michael is Christ." In putting
forward his view of events (which is also the view advanced
in the *De Doctrina*), Milton is in the odd company of a
mediaeval Catholic bishop; but the theologians of his own
time seem almost wholly against him.[18] Once again, in
interpreting the first chapter of *Genesis*, the general opinion
is that all three persons of the Trinity participated in the
process of creation; the decisive role that Milton assigns to
the Son is so unusual that the awkward reservation of VII,
587–90 becomes necessary to preserve appearances.[19]
Finally, in having Christ deliver the judgment on Adam, Eve,

17 Merritt Y. Hughes, *Ten Perspectives on Milton* (New Haven
   1965), 108–11. Hughes is responsible for drawing attention to the
   relevance of Hope Travers' *The Four Daughters of God* (Bryn
   Mawr College Monographs, VI, 1907). See also Patrides, *Milton
   and the Christian Tradition* (Oxford 1966), 24. T. M. Greene in
   The Descent from Heaven (New Haven 1963), 175, observes in
   another connection that the first person addresses the second in
   Folengo's *L'Umanita dei Figliuol di Dio* (1533).

18 *Works*, XV, 105; Grant McColley, "Milton's Battle in Heaven and
   Rupert of St. Heribert," *Speculum*, XVI (1941), 230–5; *Paradise
   Lost and the Seventeenth Century Reader*, 146–7, n. 20.

19 Elnathan Parr observes that "Creation is a Worke proper onely to
   God, undividedly common to the Father, the Sonne, and to the
   Holy Ghost." *The Ground of Divinitie* (London; date defaced),
   73. To the same effect see James Ussher, *A Body of Divinitie*
   (8th ed., London 1702), 82–3. William Ames goes so far as to say
   that "By the *Creation*, God is known, but not God the Father,
   Sonne and Holy Spirit, because that effecting power whereby the
   world was created, pertains to the essence of God and not to his
   personal subsistence." *The Marrow of Sacred Divinitie* (London
   1642), 35.

and the Serpent, Milton is, as far as we know, being unique.[20]

Explanations can be offered for each of these individualities; but the one explanation which unifies them all is that Milton is determined to have Christ and Satan emerge as dramatic antagonists in the struggle of contraries which gives the poem its energy. It is an intention which emerges not simply in the shaping but also in the placing of Christ's victories. Thus in the two assemblies, Christ's redemptive mission follows immediately on Satan's destructive design. The Creation is carefully located in the poem to be succeeded almost at once by the undoing of the creation. Christ's victory in Heaven is not as the leader of an army but single-handed, against the background of a military stalemate, the mounting violence of which threatens even the fabric of Heaven with anarchy. Thus like every act of Christ, it too is an exercise of the power of creation, opening out into the Creation which is to follow. In Christ's giving of the judgment it is subtly put to us that he is the ground as well as the instrument of order. He may be an actor in the scheme of things, but he is also the force that encloses the action. It is no accident that the affirmation of the pattern comes at a time when Sin and Death are to be unloosed on the universe. Thus at point after point in the struggle cf contraries, we are kept aware both of the form of the struggle and of its agents.

A Renaissance critic's feelings can be understood if he complains of strangulation by the Great Chain of Being. If the figure is discussed here it is because it is necessary to show how every resource in *Paradise Lost* is made to point into the centre of decision. Sin is a violation of degree and while the violation may be upwards or downwards,[21] the result of the sin can only be downwards, a tearing away of

20 D. Taylor Jr., "Milton's Treatment of the Judgement and the Expulsion in *Paradise Lost*," *Tulane Studies in English*, x (1960), 71.
21 Arnold Stein, *Answerable Style* (Minneapolis 1953), 116.

the sinful creature from the shaping principle of its own
identity. One of Raphael's earliest acts is to explain what
Adam himself calls the Scale of Nature. In doing so he also
puts before us the concept of "bounds / Proportiond to each
kind." Satan's sin, shortly to be recounted, is a breaking of
his bounds and the reader is surely meant to recall how "one
slight bound high over leap'd all bound" when the force of
destruction made its entry into Paradise.[22] For that matter,
Raphael's simile of the plant is meant to be remembered by
the attentive when we come to the imagery of redemption in
the last book.

Ulysses can speak passionately of degree in that great
speech which none of us can promise not to quote. But
Shakespeare's play is not about degree in quite the same way
as Milton's poem. Degree is part of the cosmography of
Paradise Lost and perhaps goes behind even that; the very
act of creation is a setting of bounds and the drawing of the
world's "just Circumference." (VII, 230–1; 166–7) The
golden chain evokes the Scale of Nature; and the chain and
the causeway point to the way up and the way down in the
architecture of both space and being. Reason and passion
and flesh and spirit are two of the contraries which the chain
traditionally couples. Because they meet in the mixed nature
of man we are conscious of all the other contraries that
Milton assembles, as involved in the struggle to preserve and
refine that nature. To sum up, the chain is used structurally
rather than evocatively. There is no other example in English
literature of so fundamental and far-reaching a usage.

Aristotle, in speaking tentatively of the unity of time,
says that while tragedy endeavours as far as possible to
confine itself to a single circuit of the sun, the epic action is
"not restricted to any fixed limit of time." Minturno suggests
that the length should not exceed one year. The actions of
the *Iliad* and the *Odyssey* have been reckoned as taking

22 V, 506–12; V, 477–9; IV, 181; III, 80–4, acquires new meaning
  against this background.

forty-five and forty-two days; that of *Paradise Lost* has been estimated to take precisely a month.[23] The statistics, which are of no great consequence in anyone's response to any of these poems, are quoted to suggest that the main action of *Paradise Lost* is really extraordinarily concise, reflecting the dramatic origins of the poem. Indeed, shorn of its first three books, the epic would strikingly resemble *Adam Unparadized*. But the central action is widened in time by a flashback and a movement forward (both epic devices and both neatly arranged in two courses of angelic instruction), just as it is widened in space by the two assemblies (again an epic device) and by the scope of the opening movement from darkness to light. These thrusts of expansion are unprecedented in their extent and, in combination with the confined setting of the crisis, they produce the impression for which Milton was always striving – the infinite structure encircling the infinitesimal nucleus. Perhaps it should be added that the beginning in *medias res* (another epic device) situates us on the circumference while directing our attention to the centre, whereas the Satanic voyage (still another epic device, Miltonically inverted) transports us to the centre through what is by now a cosmos of meanings as well as a physical universe.[24]

Milton's use of the resources of the *genre* is necessarily selective and having asked himself "whether the rules of Aristotle are herein to be kept or nature to be followed" he did what was right for the poem, to the distress of some neo-classical critics. The property of the epic on which he concentrates unerringly is what Aristotle called its "capacity

23 *Poetics*, 5; Lane Cooper, *Aristotle on the Art of Poetry* (rev. ed., Ithaca 1947), 15; *Literary Criticism: Plato to Dryden*, ed. W. H. Gilbert (New York 1940), 275; Grant McColley, *Paradise Lost* (Chicago 1940), 16–17.

24 The best available account of Milton's use of space is in Roy Daniells' *Milton, Mannerism and Baroque* (Toronto 1963), 87–99. See also Jackson I. Cope, *The Metaphoric Structure of Paradise Lost* (Baltimore 1962).

for extension" (*Poetics*, 24). In so doing he takes to its theo-
retical limit Aristotle's view that "so long as the plot is
perspicuous throughout, the greater the length of the story,
the more beautiful will it be on account of its magnitude
(*Poetics*, 7), with the difference that the concept of magni-
tude is applied to the total rather than to the primary action.

In creating the artifice of eternity, Milton joins many
things together and it is a personal as well as a public inheri-
tance that we see coming to fruition in his poem. The
Nativity Ode has the same panoramic movements through
time and space that distinguish the epic and, in both poems,
the lines of force reach into and radiate from a centre care-
fully confined in time and space. The centre in the *Ode* is one
of meaning; in *Paradise Lost* it is a centre of decision in
which meaning can either be preserved or undone. These
differences put it to us that the *œuvre*, in achieving that
fuller statement which is beyond the power of any single
poem, must display both variety and wholeness. In *Comus*
likewise, the theme of temptation is given its first enactment;
light and darkness, vice and virtue, flesh and spirit, chastity
and lust are brought together in a marshalling of contraries
that anticipates *Paradise Lost*,[25] just as the catalogue of false
gods in the *Ode* paves the way for the grimmer pageant of
the epic. It is of course some distance from Comus to Satan
or for that matter from Comus to Belial. The single episode
grows into the long narrative of corruption. The "curious
taste" of misrule darkens into evil, engendering and devour-
ing itself, a conception which the masque affirms but does
not reach out to embody. The well-known comparison be-
tween Comus ravished by the lady's singing and Satan
"Stupidly good" as he contemplates Eve (*Comus*, 243–63;
PL, IX, 465), is exact in the differentiation which it also

25 See in this connection John C. Demaray, "The Thrones of Satan
and God: Backgrounds to Divine Opposition in *Paradise Lost*,"
HLQ, XXXI (1967), 21–33 and esp. 27. Dr. Demaray's essay ap-
peared after this paper was written.

suggests. What is taking place is not simply development; it is, in addition, the choosing of the right *genre* at the right time by the creative talent coming into possession of its own depths. We are asked to note the expert and supple observances of "bounds proportion'd to each kind" and to discern how these observances contribute to a fuller statement of the unfolding theme. Thus in *Comus*, the place of decision is a place of confinement, looking forward beyond *Paradise Lost* to the almost claustrophobic confinements of *Samson Agonistes*. But the differences must be weighed with the similarities; the immediate setting for the crisis is a forest of deceit rather than a garden of order and the contrast is designed to suggest to us that whatever the environment, we cannot escape the ordeal. The Epilogue to *Comus* uses the garden to establish the peace of the poem, the settlement in symbol of its intellectual issues; *Paradise Lost* uses it as the focal point of the poem's war of energies. It is a war which cannot be avoided, whatever the position chosen or fortifications built. "Within himself," says Adam to Eve, "The danger lies, yet lies within his power." (IX, 348–9) So the infinite theatre narrows to the enclosure of decision and the enclosure in turn contracts to the kernel of choice in the mind.

In this way Milton's own literary past, like everything else that he inherits, is taken up into his poem providing him with his seminal oppositions, his characteristic strategies, his opening out of the meaning in time and space and with that central situation which he was repeatedly to explore and never to exhaust. The result is not monotony but a growing sense of the richness of a centre which can respond creatively to the different styles of insight regulated by the propensities of each *genre*. We also recognize, to return for a moment to Milton's heaven, that a contemplative presentation would have been foreign to his temperament. *The Nativity Ode* is a celebration of the power of the word; it rejoices not simply in goodness but in goodness at work in the redemption of history. In *Comus* for all its platonic apparatus, virtue is not simply reached up to by the aspiring mind but is held in battle against a plausible opponent. Milton's concern throughout is not with what the ultimate radiance is but with what it does and with how we are to respond to what it does. Given such a concern, the choice of a narrative form is all but inevitable; and while the form in its fullness contains introspective elements it seems unsafe to withdraw it wholly into these elements. *Paradise Lost* is a poem of the mind but it is also a poem of the mind's place in history and reality.

So far, our attention has been given to the web in its enmeshing and controlled intricacy and to those strong lines of convergence that direct the mind's eye along the web to its centre. It is time to inquire about the centre itself. At the point where all threads join we have neither a prisoner nor a manipulator, neither the spider nor the fly in marmalade. "Sufficient to have stood, though free to fall" (III, 99) is the phrase most expressive of those mixed potentialities that flow from man's mixed nature. It is expressive even in the see-saw of its balance upon the fulcrum of its own caesura. Significantly the phrase is used both of the angels and of man. On that height above all heights where past, present, and future are seen together (and where the fall of man is described in all three tenses), it is natural that we should be made aware of the universalities of freedom rather than of its accidents.

In his speech from the throne God, as might be expected, quotes the Bible frequently (a chronological purist might say that he provides a preview of it) and Sims cites no less than ninety-nine allusions in lines 80 to 342 of BOOK III.[26] This is not Milton's highest degree of allusiveness, for in BOOK XII the reminiscences are even more thick-sown and as many as fifteen references to the scriptures are made in the opening

26 James H. Sims, *The Bible in Milton's Epics* (Gainesville 1962), 261–2.

thirteen lines of the poem.[27] Nevertheless the frequency of citation in BOOK III, combined with the imaginative context, put it strongly to us that we have reached the word itself, beyond which it is impossible to look. The scriptures may be an accommodation of truth to the understanding, but the very fact of accommodation indicates that we have arrived at a boundary. We may realize that the ultimate metaphor is a metaphor; but we cannot go behind what the metaphor reveals. Both the view of truth that was typical in Milton's time and the dramatic circumstances of God's statement make it evident that we are being confronted with the *données* of the poem, the conditions on which we are enabled to enter its universe. It is therefore all the more striking that lines 87–135, in which freedom is defined in relation to foreknowledge, contain only one biblical reference and that in lines 156–66, which set the stage for the whole process of redemption, the poetry speaks for itself without biblical support.[28] Milton is not alone in his view of the nature of man's freedom (or more correctly the freedom of intelligence), but the vehemence with which the view is urged and the cosmic elevation he accords it are unique. If the tactics are not quite successful it is because in the last analysis, Milton is unable to proclaim the absolute without justifying the absolute to the relative. "The hidden ways of his providence we adore and search not," he says unexpectedly, in *The Doctrine and Discipline of Divorce*, but *Paradise Lost* is distinguished more by searching than by adoration.[29]

God's affirmation of man's freedom is sometimes too

27 Sims, 271–3, 10–11.
28 Sims, 262.
29 *Prose Works*, II, 292. The text in the background is Rom. II, 33. Luther in commenting on it says, "It is not for us to inquire into these mysteries, but to adore them." His subsequent answer to the question "Why did God let Adam fall?" is on the same lines and is in sharp contrast to *PL*. ("The Bondage of the Will," in *Martin Luther, Selections from his Writings*, ed. John Dillenberger, New York 1961, 195.) We should remember however that Milton's position on free will was closer to Luther's at the time he wrote the divorce tracts than it was when he wrote *Paradise Lost*.

strenuous to be convincing but when Raphael takes up the
theme the vehemence moderates. We approach that quiet
pride in responsibility which for Milton is part of the dignity
of man. (v, 520–8)

> That thou art happie, owe to God;
> That thou continu'st such, owe to thy self,
> That is, to thy obedience; therein stand.
> This was that caution giv'n thee; be advis'd.
> God made thee perfet, not immutable;
> And good he made thee, but to persevere
> He left it in thy power, ordain'd thy will
> By nature free, not over-rul'd by Fate
> Inextricable, or strict necessity.

Changelessness is the quality traditionally associated with
perfection. If change is for the better, that which changes
must be less than perfect. If it is for the worse, then that
which changes has within it the seeds of corruption and is
therefore imperfect. When Milton tells us that man is made
perfect rather than immutable, is he telling us that the peril
of mutability is a price worth paying for the gift of freedom
and that perfection must contain within itself the power to
alter and indeed to destroy itself? It is a daring thought
indeed and, taken in conjunction with God's setting aside of
the Bible in the third book, the thought seems renewed
evidence of Milton's determination to give the highest
conceivable status to freedom. To relinquish such an inter-
pretation is not easy but the probabilities are that Milton
meant something less.

The fact is that there are two kinds of perfection discussed
in *Paradise Lost*. The perfection of the creator is changeless.
That of the created, however, must be involved in change if
it is to proceed up the scale of nature within the bounds
proportioned to its kind.[30] When we come to the perfection

30 On Milton's relative use of perfection see Ogden, 6, and Ruth Mohl,
   Studies in Spenser, Milton and the Theory of Monarchy (New York
   1949), 125–6.

of intelligence, the possibility must be faced of movement both upwards and downwards. Freedom of decision is part of the dignity of the higher creation and the price of that freedom is exposure to the risk of mutability. "Reason also is choice" God tells us in the third book, echoing a phrase from *Areopagitica* on virtue militant, as well as Pico's recognition of man's unique capacity to make or unmake himself.[31] We are also being told that since man, like all created things, is involved in the time-process, the nature of man can only be completed in action. The highest form of action is responsible action and responsible action can only result from a freedom which includes the power to act otherwise. For this freedom, mutability, the great defections of history and the blood of the redemption are the cosmic prices which omniscience knows will be paid. The toll that is exacted is a testimony both stern and compassionate to the significance of the gift bestowed upon us.

If reason is choice, it is also more than choice. "What obeyes / Reason, is free" and not to obey reason is to be trapped in selfhood: "Thy self not free but to thy self enthrall'd." (IX, 351–2; VI, 181) But error can seem reasonable in *Paradise Lost* and reason can seem to be arbitrary. The dark wood of our condition is considerably more perplexing than the forest in *Comus* where enchanters who have shown themselves to be treacherous offer charmed draughts to ladies they have imprisoned. In *Paradise Lost*, the devil's party consists of heroic democrats, gallant minorities resisting murderous force, and serpents rising through the scale of nature upon the elegant coils of classical myth. The poem judges these pretences if it is read alertly, but there are times when Milton, far from avoiding the confusion of appearances, seems intent on adding to it, perhaps as a test of the reader's vigilance. The prohibition against eating the fruit is in the Bible and cannot be escaped from; but the unexplained exaltation of the Son at the beginning of celes-

31 "The Constant Core," *East-West Review*, III (1967), 122.

tial history is neither in the Bible, nor in tradition,[32] nor in the *De Doctrina*, and is therefore a difficulty which Milton chose to make for himself. To anyone sensitive to the larger symmetries of *Paradise Lost*, it is apparent that one purpose of this "invention" is to tie together the angelic and human falls and to link them within a circle that begins and ends with the exaltation of the Son. But though the pattern may be strengthened, we are also made sharply aware by the parallelism that the two falls proceed from divine decrees which are left unexplained. Substance is given to the argument that the universe that Milton is creating is a universe of *diktat* rather than reason.

The issue has been isolated as clearly as possible and Milton criticism is certainly adept enough to be capable of offering more than one explanation. It can be argued that Milton, the supreme structuralist, was prepared to pay the price for his pattern and that the price he paid shows the importance of the pattern. More popular would be the view that even Milton with his powers of artistic unification is not always fully in command of the varied resources that inhabit his poem. There are times when the totalitarian nature of his deity, or to put it more blandly, the force of cosmic will, breaks through the containment of Christian humanism which the poem is so earnestly seeking to erect.[33] The best explanation is perhaps the least persuasive when it

32 The view that the disclosure of the Incarnation occasioned the rebellion in Heaven (Williams, *The Common Expositor*, 118; McColley, *Paradise Lost*, 32–3) may have provided Milton with the basis for his "invention," but is not the same thing as the invention itself.

33 Daniells, who regards will as the axis of Milton's universe (*Milton, Mannerism and Baroque*, 64–86), finds this fact indicative of Baroque achievement rather than artistic failure. Perhaps it can be argued that a universe built round the primacy of the divine will is Augustinian as much as it is baroque. Herschel Baker notes for instance that "Augustine's radical departure from the humanistic tradition is apparent in his substituting of will for reason in his hierarchy of values." *The Image of Man* (1961 ed.), 172.

is first offered. The infinite will always seem inscrutable in its crucial dealings with the finite. Expressed in decrees, the inscrutable will seem arbitrary. The correct response is not to recoil in rebellion at the apparent arbitrariness, but to answer the will of God with the whole being of the mind. Even in the prelapsarian world there are things which cannot be understood until they are accepted. Acceptance indeed creates the relationship out of which alone understanding can flow. Rejection is a turning away from God and the subtlest form of turning away is that which professes to forsake God for reason. Proclaiming the free intelligence as its standard, it is none the less profoundly unintelligent. This is the great paradox of temptation: the declaration of independence and selfhood, which is in reality the testament of servitude, and the spontaneous acceptance of dependence, which is the discovery of the self in filial freedom.

Reason to the seventeenth century was an ethical and religious rather than an intellectual concept.[34] Right reason is the candle of the Lord. When God crowns his creation with the "Master work," he brings into being a creature endowed with "Sanctitie of Reason." (VII, 511–13)[35]

> Magnanimous to correspond with Heav'n,
> But grateful to acknowledge whence his good
> Descends ...

The moral connotations of reason are evident elsewhere. Love has its seat in reason. The "mysterious Law" of wedded love is founded in reason "Loyal, Just and Pure." Whether discursive or intuitive, reason is, Raphael tells us, the "being" of the Soul, and reason, according to Michael, is virtue. (VIII, 589–92; IV, 750–7; V, 483–8; XII, 98) But because rea-

34 A fuller discussion of the concept than is possible here will be found in R. A. Hoopes, *Right Reason in the English Renaissance* (Camb., Mass. 1962).
35 Christ in *PR* exemplifies the whole of this description and not simply its first line.

son is part of the image of God in man, it is only right reason
when it is founded in righteousness. (IV, 291–5)[36]

> in thir looks Divine
> The Image of thir glorious Maker shon,
> Truth, Wisdome, Sanctitude severe and pure,
> Severe, but in true filial freedom plac't;
> Whence true autoritie in men ...

"Reasons mintage" remains as in *Comus*, "Character'd in
the face" (528–9), but whereas reason in Milton's masque
was set within chastity, reason in *Paradise Lost* is set within
moral completeness. Filial freedom supersedes the freedom
which flowed from the love of virtue. The more explicit ter-
minology suggests no difference in kind; indeed the severity
and purity with which truth, wisdom, and sanctitude are
invested may well be regarded as chastity reborn. What is
taking place is the restatement of a familiar Miltonic con-
cern: the relationship between discipline and liberty pro-
claimed on this occasion, as the indwelling presence of the
image of God in man.

The divine image in the human countenance expresses
the perfection of man. But man's perfection, like every finite

36 The nature of the image of God in man is discussed by Williams
in *The Common Expositor*, 72–5. The image is both inward and
outward. Outwardly, the image is expressed in Adam's dominion
over the creatures (as in VIII, 540–6), and according to some com-
mentators, in Adam's dominion over Eve. The inward image is
found, to quote Ussher's typical wording, in "the perfection of his
[Adam's] Nature, indued with Reason and Will, rightly disposed
in Holiness and Righteousness, Wisdom and Truth; and accord-
ingly framing all Motions and Actions, both inward and out-
ward." *A Body of Divinitie*, 92. See also Elnathan Parr, *The
Grounds of Divinitie*, 122, and William Ames, *The Marrow of
Sacred Divinitie* (London 1642), 38. Milton describes the image
as consisting of "Wisdom, Purity, Justice, and rule over all crea-
tures." (*Prose Works*, II, 587) In *PL*, he is not only providing a
description of the inward image, but suggesting in line 295 that
the outer image depends upon the inner.

perfection, can only complete itself by reaching outside itself. The remarkable dialogue between God and Adam which Milton invents has more than one purpose; it suggests for example that Christ's function as mediator becomes necessary only after the Fall; and since even the loyal Abdiel is not addressed so directly, the dignity of man is subtly emphasized. But the principal aim of the incident is to tell us of the circumstances of Eve's creation. Unfortunately, the argument of VIII, 412–26 can scarcely be called a model of lucidity. Perhaps Yeats, whether or not he had read this particular passage, seizes the essence of it in telling us that "we beget and bear because of the incompleteness of our love."[37] God is perfect, deficient in nothing, containing within his unity every possible multiplicity. Man can only extend his finiteness by joining it in love to a complementary finiteness. The word "extends" is important. Adam is not meant to complete himself *in* Eve, and when he decides to do so he has fallen. Rather, he is meant to complete himself *with* Eve. The two enrich each other only as the dependence on God enriches them both. When the supporting relationship is abandoned, the auxiliary relationship which it sanctifies becomes engrossed in itself and wrenched away from reality. We remember then that the birth of Eve recalls the birth of Sin, even in the springing into life from the left side.[38]

In his account of the Fall, Milton faces peculiar difficulties.

37 *The Letters of W. B. Yeats*, ed. Allan Wade (New York 1955), 824.
38 *Gen.* II, 21–2, does not mention the side from which Eve was created. Davis P. Harding, in pointing out how the birth of Sin diabolically distorts the birth of Pallas Athene, notes that "on the theory that the rib from which Eve was fashioned must have been extracted from a region near Adam's heart, most commentators had concluded that the rib was taken from the left side. Milton apparently subscribed to this view. But, so far as I have been able to discover, no mythographer had ever designated the side of the head from which Pallas Athene was born. Milton, very likely, therefore, invented this detail." *The Club of Hercules* (Urbana 1962), 75.

It is not easy to differentiate dramatically freedom to fall from a propensity for falling, or to paint a vulnerability which is short of being a defect. The many poems and plays on the subject bypass the problem by not going behind the event. Milton is unique in his readiness to explore what has to be called the psychology of Adam and Eve. It is an exploration which is lengthened and given additional complexity by narrative flashbacks, by dreams which are also omens, by specific warnings not simply of the danger, but of the detailed shape of temptation, which those who receive them are persuaded to ignore, by probing dialogues between guide and learner in the cosmic hierarchy which set forth the principles of right action, and finally, by the style itself, by the allusions arching across the web, reaching backwards into the literary past and forward into the history of the poem. So sustained is this process that many of us react to it as a slowly accelerating slippage so that the eating of the fruit is merely the point at which the gathering weight begins to avalanche. The image is suggestive but not wholly reliable. The breakaway in the self can be pulled back and the forces which are involved in it are not so much forces of weakness as forces capable of good within their bounds. Reason and self-restraint can recognize and arrest the slippage. They have more than one opportunity to do so. When they fail to act, a point is reached when they can no longer act. The rash hand reaches out to rend the web and the self tears itself away from its position in reality.

No one denies that Adam and Eve are free to fall, but some suggest that they are insufficient to have stood. Our courts of law refuse very rightly to accept from those made in Adam's image the plea that they could not refrain from what they knew to be wrong; but the same plea is mysteriously more convincing when it is invoked for those made in the image of God. Some realism seems to be needed here. Eve's rehearsal of her sin in her dream is sufficiently detailed to put her on her guard; the ease with which she passes from

"damp horror"[39] at the possibility of eating the fruit to ex-
hilaration in the eating of it is more than fair warning. But
her self-esteem, innocent in the Narcissus episode, becomes
grounded in rather less than just and right, to quote Ra-
phael's vain recommendation to Adam. In the separation
scene in the ninth book she is militantly self-confident, cer-
tain of her power to defeat her adversary and insistent on
sallying forth to meet him.[40] Adam's sedate advice that two
heads are better than one and that there is trouble enough
even in Paradise without our looking for it falls on an unre-
ceptive mind. Even his laboriously diplomatic suggestion
that the prospective assault on Eve's righteousness is an in-
sult she should not be asked to endure, proves unavailing.
Satan is far more practised at winning his way into the
lady's heart. Eve is sufficient to have stood with Adam. She
becomes insufficient when she deems herself more than
sufficient.

If Eve is left unprotected in any way, it is by Adam's de-
sertion of his hierarchical function. His learned lecture on
psychology after Eve's dream evades the warning which he
ought to deliver. In the debate on collective security he capi-
tulates abruptly, serving notice of the more serious capitula-
tion which is soon to come. His parting advice to Eve is to
let her reason beware lest "She dictate false, and misinforme
the Will / To do what God expressly hath forbid." (IX,
355–6) The caution has its relevance, but the blunter warn-
ing against Eve seeking to rise above her position in the
scale of nature is not provided, perhaps because Adam him-
self is more than inclined to deify Eve. Adam's other state-
ments that the will is truly free only in obedience to reason
and that the real danger to man comes from within become
even more searching when they are directed against himself.

39 V, 65. Note the echo at IX, 890.
40 Eve's Areopagitican argument is not employed inconsistently or
   absent-mindedly. See Arnold Williams, "Eve, the Devil and
   Areopagitica," MLQ, V (1944), 429–34.

Adam's testing is more severe than that of Eve. He has to choose between two loyalties and the depth of the lesser loyalty is measured by his curious and touching suggestion that something of his essential self was subtracted in the making of Eve. He is perfect man with one flaw designed into him; weakness "Against the charm of Beauties powerful glance." (VIII, 530–7) Lines VIII, 540–6, make it clear that he is aware of Eve's real position on the ladder of being. But the lines that follow make it even clearer that when he approaches her loveliness, the minor brilliance overwhelms the true light. The very language of the exaltation, the emphasis on Eve's absoluteness and self-sufficiency, recall with saddening exactness Adam's recognition of God's nature in 414–16. The climactic displacement is that in addressing an angel, Adam should speak of an angelic guard surrounding the presence of Eve.

The angel, not unnaturally, answers "with contracted brow." (VIII, 560) Nothing essential, he tells Adam, has been taken from his nature; it is merely that he is in danger of being unduly swayed by his emotions. Those who find this judgment harsh are perhaps in a worse plight than Adam, for Adam himself admits that he is fully capable of discerning and choosing the good. (VIII, 607–11)

> I to thee disclose
> What inward thence I feel, not therefore foild,
> Who meet with various objects, from the sense
> Variously representing; yet still free
> Approve the best, and follow what I approve.

Later, in saying farewell to Eve, Adam returns to that crucial statement in VIII, 414–16, this time expressing correctly the mirroring of God's perfection in the finite perfection of man. (IX, 343–9)

> O Woman, best are all things as the will
> Of God ordain'd them, his creating hand

Nothing imperfet or deficient left
Of all that he Created, much less Man,
Or aught that might his happie State secure,
Secure from outward force; within himself
The danger lies, yet lies within his power.

Adam is recorded as speaking these words "fervently,"
which presumably means that his convictions lie behind
them. Soon after he has spoken them, the edifice of perfec-
tion lies in ruins, overwhelmed by the danger within. The
breakaway from the greater to the lesser love takes place
with feverish celerity. It requires only eight lines for Adam
to proceed from his shocked recognition of Eve's plight –
"How art thou lost, how on a sudden lost" – to his desperate
decision to share her fate (IX, 900–7). "Certain my resolution
is to Die" is a declaration all the more telling because it is
not until the eleventh book that Adam learns the meaning of
death. The imagery has its own comment to make, for even
before Adam begins to speak the garland he has wreathed
for Eve has withered. We realize that the poem too has its
own ways of foreknowledge and its sense of freedom be-
trayed within that knowledge. Later when Adam begins to
rationalize his decision, he uses in IX, 943–8 precisely the
argument that Christ uses in the dialogue in heaven.[41] Adam
hopes his sin will be excused. We know that it will be re-
deemed. The sacrificial gestures of romantic love are set
firmly in the context of the true sacrifice.

Literature from the nineteenth century onwards has been
largely the work of the devil's party, but even readers whose
affiliations are different may feel the bond of nature drawing
them to Adam. The poetry allows us to make this identifica-
tion. It also demands that we draw back from it and judge it.
It is the double response which causes difficulty, encourag-
ing critics to argue that the poetry is once again fatally un-

41 III, 150–64. A double connection is at work, for IX, 901, recalls
III, 208.

balanced, with the intellectual plan at variance with the imaginative accomplishment. But the movement of judgment is unmistakable and is enforced by the poetry itself, rather than by the author's pointing finger. To go behind Adam's own metaphor, the forging of the link is the breaking of the chain and the sealing of the bond tears a greater bond to pieces.[42] It does not take long for wedded love to become lust, and for Eve no longer "blushing like the Morn" to look on Adam with eyes that dart "contagious Fire" (recalling Satan's eyes that "sparkling blaz'd").[43] The creative energy of nature "boon" and wantoning as in her prime was earlier metamorphosed into the destructive energy of Eve "hight'nd as with Wine jocond and boon." (IV, 241–3; V, 294–7; IX, 792–3) Even more pointed in its valuation is the manner in which Adam is made to surrender to Eve. The separate temptations which Milton employs are, as has been shown earlier, part of his understanding of the nature of tempta-tion, but by giving Eve permission to leave Adam not only makes possible the encounter in solitude, but also reiterates his weakness and assumes responsibility for what is to fol-low.[44] After Eve has succumbed alone, she plucks a bough from the tree and takes it with her. No commentator on *Genesis* seems to have thought of making her do this;[45] the

42 IX, 913–14; 955–6. Death's remarks in X, 243–51, with their specific echo of X, 1010 are a grim commentary on the real nature of the link.

43 VIII, 511; IX, 1036; I, 193–4; see also II, 386–8; IX, 1036, it will be observed, develops the destructive implications of VIII, 532–3. Williams (*The Common Expositor*, 84) says that Milton in speak-ing of wedded love before the Fall "is going farther than most of the commentators warrant." McColley (*Paradise Lost*, 178) de-scribes as distinctly uncommon the idea that there was lustful intercourse in Paradise after the Fall. Once again Milton breaks with tradition to achieve an important contrast.

44 Analyses of this scene are not lacking. For one particularly rele-vant to the view expressed here see Dennis H. Burden, *The Logical Epic* (London 1967), 80–93.

45 Milton's originality in this detail was pointed out to me by Pro-fessor Svendsen.

result is that instead of Adam being brought to the tree, the tree is as it were brought to Adam. Nothing could exemplify more tellingly Adam's complete abdication from his functions of guidance and judgment. Adam then decides to share Eve's fate, Eve commends him lavishly, and he passes into sin with her: (IX, 995–7)

> from the bough
> She gave him of that fair enticing Fruit
> With liberal hand ...

Genesis III, 6 and 12, provide a foundation here, but the liberal hand plying the passive Adam and the bough which Eve has thoughtfully brought to the banquet put her somewhat masculine aggressiveness ("Forth reaching to the Fruit, she pluck't, she eat") in studied contrast to Adam's dazed and feminine acquiescence. The hierarchic roles have been reversed. "The Feete must guide and direct the head," was Goodman's disgusted comment.[46] It might almost be said that Adam has regressed into infantility with Eve as his nursemaid. More examples of this implicit commentary could be given, and the moral is not simply that we should read the poem with care. Even when the conclusion is explicit as in IX, 997–9, the difference between the spontaneous and the directed response does not necessarily mean that the author's imagination has run away with him and that he is pursuing the poem vainly crying "Stop, thief!" Rather, we are being invited to read the passage again. When we do so, our sense of the gap ought to alter. As our understandings grow up to the demand that is made upon them, we learn more about the poem and possibly more about ourselves.[47]

At the centre of the web is the nucleus of freedom. But freedom must be set in a constellation of significance sug-

46 Godfrey Goodman, *The Fall of Man* (London 1616), 429.
47 This view is similar to that put forward in detail and with subtlety by Stanley E. Fish in *Surprised by Sin* (London 1967). See also pages xxvi–xxviii of the introduction to the present author's edition of the first two books of *PL* (Bombay 1964).

gested partly by the web itself. It finds its nature in obedience to reason and in creative rootedness in the order of things. It extends itself in relationships which complete themselves in God. It is responsibility, obedience, and guidance. It is the energy to act, curbed by the knowledge that sanctitude invests the power of choice. Its context is blood, imagination, and intellect running together in devotion to the good. It brings to perfection the finite creature which it animates but the perfection consists of the power to walk a tightrope and when concentration relaxes the abyss opens. The mandate which Raphael is given conveys some of the feeling of this perilous privilege. (v, 233–7)

> such discourse bring on
> As may advise him of his happie state,
> Happiness in his power left free to will
> Left to his own free Will, his Will though free,
> Yet mutable ...

There is a tentativeness here, a hovering in the verse, which seems expressive of the knowledge that freedom can make more than one thing of itself. The repetitions give additional weight to the concept; but they also seem to turn it around, exposing its various facets to the light. The undercutting effect of "though" and "yet," carefully positioned at the climax of insistence, is confirmed as the force of the thought comes to rest paradoxically on the word "mutable." It is the price that has to be paid not for perfection but for human perfection; and as the forces of the fable and of Milton's powerfully organized arrangement of it mass themselves around the precarious centre, we cannot but be made intensely aware of the price.

Sin and Wisdom spring fully armed, from the mind. Hell is a place, but within it lives a person whose fate is to discover that he himself is hell. Johnson spoke disparagingly of the confusion of spirit and matter in *Paradise Lost*,[48] but

48 *Johnson's Life of Milton*, ed. C. H. Firth (Oxford 1888), 76.

perhaps the critic of today can see that one of the principal strengths of the poem is its fluency of movement between the interior and the outer world, so that each is an affirmation of the other and both lead to the consummation of the paradise within. The forces of the poem have moved inwards on the garden; now they erupt outwards from the violating nexus, stamping the deformity of misgovernment on the new nature of things. The interconnectedness which the poem has assiduously built up is now seen to mean that all falls apart when the centre fails to hold. The tenth book is concerned with the expansion of sin into space and the eleventh and twelfth books with its expansion into history. Yet as we are caught up in the momentum of this reversal, the crumbling of a great edifice exposed to the waywardness of freedom, we become aware that there is more to be said. Good comes out of evil and what providence achieves is not what the agent intends. Adam and Eve seek godhead and find debasement. Satan proclaims his new empire and chews the bitter ashes of his victory. The fallen angels debate upon a hill and find no end in the wandering mazes of philosophy. Adam is led through mazes to the admission of his own guilt. He ascends a different hill from which he sees both sin and salvation. The face of things may alter, but the pulsation of things continues. Behind appearance and even behind experience, we are required to remain aware of the divine plan and its controlling ironies. Book Ten indeed is built on two dramatic contrasts between what is of present and what is of future significance. The eating of the fruit takes place against an inclusive and intricate statement of order, an order sufficiently comprehensive to draw into its scope energy, passion, and movement. The repentance of Adam and Eve, their "Sorrow unfeign'd, and humiliation meek" (x, 1092; 1104) takes place against a proliferating chaos, a declaration of war within and between things. Both acts are insignificant against their cosmic backgrounds and both tell us that insignificance is significant. Together they outline the condition of man.

"The War of Mankind with the Devil," Ussher informs us, "is a lawful War, proclaimed of God, which is also perpetual and without any Truce."[49] If fallen man fights this war, it is wholly by virtue of a power that is given him, a power which he can neither turn to nor repudiate. He is in truth a battlefield rather than a centre of choice. Good and evil contend for his soul; but if he is able to choose the good, it is only because the good has previously chosen him. In Luther's harsh and telling words:

Man's will is like a beast standing between two riders.
If God rides, it wills and goes where God wills ...
If Satan rides, it wills and goes where Satan wills
Nor may it choose to which rider it will run, or which
it will seek; but the riders themselves fight to decide
who shall have and hold it.[50]

Milton agreed with Luther on the location of Hell[51] and on the abolition of the Law by the Gospel.[52] It is not clear to what extent he might once have agreed with him on the bondage of the Will. He was a Trinitarian at the time of the early ecclesiastical pamphlets and appears to have been a Calvinist when he wrote Areopagitica and The Doctrine and Discipline of Divorce. (Prose Works, I, 613–14; II, 293; II, 519–20) When and for what reasons he changed to the positions held in the De Doctrina and Paradise Lost are matters which remain among the mysteries of a fairly well-documented life. To those concerned with the poetry, however,

49 Ussher, A Body of Divinitie, 123.
50 Luther, De servo arbitrio, tr. J. I. Packer and O. R. Johnson (1957), 103 ff.
51 See above, n. 14.
52 The agreement is noted by A. S. P. Woodhouse, The Poet and His Faith (Chicago 1965), 107. See in particular, Luther's Commentary on Galatians.

it will be apparent that *Comus*, written much earlier, is scarcely a Calvinist poem. When the Attendant Spirit says "Mortals that would follow me / Love vertue, she alone is free," he is not suggesting that only the chosen are capable of following him and that they, having been chosen, are incapable of not following. In fact, the prolonged drama of temptation with which Milton was persistently (and some might say obstinately) concerned would not be very much of a drama if the man at the centre could only prefer what he was elected or condemned to prefer. Predestination may be grimly edifying but it has its deficiencies as a poetic spectacle.

These considerations, as might be expected, apply with particular force to *Paradise Lost*. The entire cosmic mobilization has been massed around and made to converge upon an active, choosing centre. The war for the soul of man is decreed by Providence within the ground-rules of man's freedom. Eliminate that freedom and the entire apparatus so laboriously and compellingly built up is reduced to irrelevance by the eating of an apple. Man can destroy himself but poems cannot. If *Paradise Lost* is to survive as an entity, fallen man cannot be entirely stripped of freedom, of some share in the making of his destiny. "The decree of Predestination," says Peter Du Moulin "is that whereby God hath appointed what he will do with us and not what he would have us do."[53] Similarly Elnathan Parr argues that "the will is no agent but a meere patient in the act of conversion to God."[54] In *Paradise Lost* though, the turn to good is not possible without prevenient grace, but prevenient grace by itself cannot ensure the turn.[55] Something in man remains to

---

53 Peter Du Moulin, *The Anatomy of Arminianism* (London 1626), 85.
54 Elnathan Parr, *The Grounds of Divinitie*, 30.
55 See X, 1–8 where prevenient grace is mentioned for the only time in the epic. Ephraim Pagitt in discussing the concept observes: "The Papists say that man's will worketh with God's grace in the first conversion of a sinner by itself: we say that man's will worketh with God's grace in the first conversion, yet not of itself

be uplifted, so that it can reach out to God. To reach out or to fall away remain possibilities within the unstable core of man's freedom. Whatever may be the dogma, the dramatic context shows us two people examining themselves, acknowledging their guilt, and taking by virtue of something in themselves the first tentative steps away from the abyss.

Arminianism was the great aberration of the early seventeenth century. By the time Thomas Edwards wrote *Gangraena* the rot had spread so far that he was prepared to admit that there were worse things than Arminianism though Arminianism itself had become considerably worse.[56] The principal threat by then was from the sectarian left rather than from the Papist right and Anabaptism was the reigning horror.[57] Nevertheless, when Little Gidding was described as an Arminian nunnery the anonymous author was joining two classic terms of Puritan invective in what was, for him, a deft compounding of insult.[58] Milton's views on free will are usually described as Arminian, an identification that has curiously gone unscrutinized, so that we look in vain for the work of scholarship on Milton and Arminius. It is a description which is fortunately less misleading than it might be. *Paradise Lost* is tactful about its theology. It is a poem designed to be read without anguish by those who do not share Milton's views. Consequently it is not always

but by grace." *Heresiography* (London 1654), 129–30. For contrasted views on the relation of grace to fallen nature see Dick Taylor Jr., "Grace as a Means of Poetry: Milton's Pattern for Salvation," *Tulane Studies in English*, IV (1954), 57, 73, and Jackson C. Boswell, "Milton and Prevenient Grace," *SEL*, VII (1967), 84–94.

56 Thomas Edwards, *Gangraena* (London 1646), 63, 74–6.

57 For the association of Arminianism with the religious right see Godfrey Davies, "Arminian versus Puritan in England, c. 1620–1650," *Huntington Library Bulletin*, V (1934), 157–79. The background of Anglo-Dutch Arminianism is succinctly discussed by Rosalie Colie in *Light and Enlightenment* (Cambridge 1957), 1–21.

58 *The Arminian Nunnery* (London 1641). The author goes on (p. 10) to describe Arminianism as a bridge to Popery and "a great part of the Clergie of this Land" as "downright Arminians."

poetically wise to nail down the letter of its dogma. What can be said is that the spirit of the poem is far closer to Arminianism (as expressed in the Remonstrance of 1610 and in contemporary understanding of the movement)[59] than it is to the Calvinist position. This is as it ought to be and if Milton decided to bid good-night to Calvin[60] it was surely in

59 See, for example, "The five articles of the Remonstrants," *Documents of the Christian Church*, ed. Henry Bettenson (London 1943), 374–6; Peter Du Moulin, *The Anatomy of Arminianism*; Ephraim Pagitt, *Heresiography*, 105–12; Alexander Ross, *A View of All Religions of the World* (London 1673), 367–9; Daniel Featley, *Pelagius Redivivus* (London 1626). A synthesized account, based on the above, might read as follows:

Christ died for all mankind and not for the elect alone. No man is doomed only for original sin. Eternal life is given to all that believe and all men are given grace and sufficient power to believe. Salvation depends on free will applying itself to grace universally offered. But grace is not irresistible. A man may hinder his own regeneration or not make use of the strength given him. Election depends on the free assent of man's will, which even with the help of saving grace may choose otherwise. (III, 173–202 is relevant here. Maurice Kelley in *PMLA*, 1937, 75–79 has shown the agreement of this passage with the *De Doctrina* and its differences from the Westminster confession.) Election may further be incomplete and the incompletely elected may become reprobate. Consequently the number of the elect is not fixed. (The Remonstrants' fifth article has misgivings at this point.) Man after the Fall is not dead in sin. He is able to thirst after righteousness. If the darkness is cleared from his understanding and his unruly affections tamed, his will is not incapable of choosing good. There is a common grace left to man after the Fall which is basically the light of nature; by good use of this common grace man can attain to evangelical or saving grace. (The bearing of these propositions on the events in BOOK X will be apparent.) In addition to a general and conditional election, there is another election of particular men whom God foresees from eternity would believe in Christ and persevere in the faith. "God hath precisely and absolutely decreed to save some certaine men, for their faith fore-seen." (Du Moulin, 114. The proposition illuminates III, 183–4.)

Milton's position on the universality of grace has affinities with that taken by Melanchthon. See *Melanchthon on Christian Doctrine*, ed. Clyde L. Manschreck (New York 1965), 60, 187–91.
60 C. A. Patrides, *Milton and the Christian Tradition* (Oxford 1966), 195; John Hales, *Golden Remains* (London 1673), Introductory letter.

the interests of the poem. Perhaps good-night was said before the poem was written. Or perhaps it was said as a result of writing the poem. It is inconceivable that a man composing an epic over ten years, fitting piece after piece into the design that his imagination insistently presented, watching the whole become incarnate in the parts and the parts find their identity in the whole, should have learned nothing at the end except how to compose an epic. At any rate, if the structure of *Paradise Lost* is not to be washed away with Paradise, it must remain in being around a certain continuity between the situations of fallen and unfallen man.

That continuity is to be found in the persistent fact of freedom. Man after the Fall is by his own act given over to darkness. But the grace of God, offered to all who turn to it, restores the balance of power, resurrects the reality of a choosing centre, and permits the mind to hold itself away from its destruction. (III, 175–9)

> Once more I will renew
> His lapsed powers, though forfeit and enthrall'd
> By sin to foul exorbitant desires;
> Upheld by me, yet once more he shall stand
> On even ground against his mortal foe.

The result is not meant to be certain victory. It is simply protection against certain defeat. Both the return to God and alienation from God lie equally within the scope of freedom. And salvation is not so much decreed as secured, won inch by inch by the cumulative exercise of the moral intelligence turning towards righteousness: (III, 193–6)

> And I will place within them as a guide
> My Umpire *Conscience*, whom if they will hear,
> Light after light well us'd they shall attain,
> And to the end persisting, safe arrive.

The divine process never quite repeats itself and the order to come may not be entirely the order that was destroyed. But body can work up to spirit both in the individual and in the possible movement of history. Man stands where he stood and knows that the web defines him. Involvement, dependence, and relationship are for him not limitations, but the outline of his nature which right action must fill in and make perfect. Responsibility is the price of freedom, but it is also the means by which freedom finds itself.

This book

was designed by

ELLEN HUTCHISON

under the direction of

ALLAN FLEMING

University of

Toronto

Press